Divine Presence

Divine Presence

An Introduction to Christian Theology

Knut Alfsvåg

WIPF & STOCK · Eugene, Oregon

DIVINE PRESENCE
An Introduction to Christian Theology

Copyright © 2021 Knut Alfsvåg. All rights reserved. Except for brief quotations in critical publications or reviews, no part of this book may be reproduced in any manner without prior written permission from the publisher. Write: Permissions, Wipf and Stock Publishers, 199 W. 8th Ave., Suite 3, Eugene, OR 97401.

Wipf and Stock Publishers
199 W. 8th Ave., Suite 3
Eugene, OR 97401

www.wipfandstock.com

PAPERBACK ISBN: 978-1-6667-0141-8
HARDCOVER ISBN: 978-1-6667-0142-5
EBOOK ISBN: 978-1-6667-0143-2

Cataloguing-in-Publication data:

Names: Alfsvåg, Knut, author.

Title: Divine presence : an introduction to Christian theology / by Knut Alfsvåg.

Description: Eugene, OR: Wipf and Stock Publishers, 2021 | Includes bibliographical references and index.

Identifiers: ISBN 978-1-6667-0141-8 (paperback) | ISBN 978-1-6667-0142-5 (hardcover) | ISBN 978-1-6667-0143-2 (ebook)

Subjects: LCSH: Theology | Christian Theology | Theology, Doctrinal | Knowledge, Theory of (Religion)

Classification: BT65 A457 2021 (print) | BT65 (ebook)

08/31/21

Scripture quotations are from the ESV* Bible (The Holy Bible, English Standard Version*), copyright © 2001 by Crossway, a publishing ministry of good News Publishers. Used by permission. All rights reserved.

Contents

Preface | vii

1. Content and method in theology | 1

FIRST PART: Theology as an academic discipline

2. The question of theological knowledge | 9
   Knowledge, truth, and justification 9
   Theological knowledge 19

3. What does it mean that the world is created? | 24
   God's unknowability 24
   The theology of modernity and its critics 31

4. What is the meaning of divine revelation? | 39
   Prophecy and incarnation 39
   The significance of Christology for the understanding of reality 46

5. How does one become a theologian? | 56
   Reasoning, self-understanding, and spirituality 56
   The doctrine of election as a problem of theological method 61
   Obedience and discipleship under modernity and postmodernity 66
   Revelation as living water and theoretical knowledge 69

SECOND PART: Sources of theological knowledge

6. The Bible as source and norm for Christian theology | 73
   The two parts of the Bible   73
   The clarity of the Scripture and historical-critical Bible research   80
   The significance of the Bible after modernity   87

7. The history and unity of the church | 90
   The catholicity of the church   90
   The plurality of doctrine and the ecumenical movement   96

8. Religious experience | 101
   Presence and anxiety   101
   Healing and liberation   108

9. Reason as a source of theological knowledge | 114
   Proofs of the existence of God?   114
   Theology and natural science   121

10. Goals and means for theological work | 128

Bibliography | 133
Index of Names | 137
Index of Subjects | 139

Preface

I have over the years taught a number of classes on the understanding of theology as an academic subject. In doing so, I have missed a textbook that situates theology in the academic context while at the same time seeing the study of theology as a means to prepare students for a ministry captured by what the apostle Paul describes as the movement "from faith for faith." I therefore found that I had to write it. This book considers the study of theology through a discussion of its relation to contemporary debates in philosophy of science while at the same time understanding both the student and the subject of theology in a way that is inspired by the spirituality of the worshipping community. Hopefully, the book will in this way contribute to bridging the repeatedly discussed and deplored gap between church and academy.

Both as a pastor and a professor I am working within a Lutheran context, and this has obviously influenced the book. At the same time, Christian theology that wants to be taken seriously should aim at catholicity in the sense this is presupposed in the Nicene Creed. My intention has therefore been to write in a way that is ecumenically relevant.

The discussions and research projects that have contributed to shaping the chapters of this book, are too numerous to count. A few indications will be given in the footnotes. The readers will find that I on several occasions have referred to some of my own books and articles, where the argument is unpacked in greater detail than what is possible in a textbook intended for a more general audience. To the part of this audience that has made up my classes during that last thirty years I am particularly grateful for the many good, and sometimes challenging, questions.

Knut Alfsvåg
Stavanger, Norway, 30 January 2021

1
Content and method in theology

ALL HUMANS HAVE A relationship to God. This is a reality both today and as far back as our sources go. These relationships are quite different, both concerning the characteristics of the God or Gods one believes or does not believe in and concerning the level of engagement of the believers or non-believers. However, it is hardly absent in the sense that one considers the question of God as totally uninteresting or completely irrelevant. Some decades ago, several scholars thought that the Western part of the world was moving towards a situation where God would be uninteresting for most people, but they were wrong. Not many would think so today.[1]

Scholarly work with the God-relationship related to the perspective of believers is called theology. The word was introduced by Plato[2] and has been used in different ways during the centuries, but today it is normally used in this sense: theology is the work of believers or non-believers on their own God-relationship with the goal of understanding its presuppositions, content, and theoretical and practical consequences. We thus have as many theologies as we have perceptions of God; we have Christian, Jewish, Muslim, Buddhist, Hindu, pantheist, animist, and atheist theology, and variations of these. Atheism belongs on the list because even atheists often have a quite involved relationship to the God they do not believe in. To understand theology as related to the perspective of (non-)believers therefore does not imply that it is an internal project for a specific fellowship of believers. Theology is an academic discipline that discusses the God-relationship as something that affects all people, since all have a positive or negative God-relationship of which they are more or less conscious.

---

1. An early and interesting literary expression of this shift of attitude was Berger, *The Desecularization of the World*.

2. Plato, *Republic*, 379a (Plato, *Complete Works*, 1017).

This book is mainly a book about *Christian* theology. Its point of departure is thus the God-relationship as understood and mediated in the Christian church through the ages and today. It is written for those who are interested in Christian theology either because they study theology preparing for church ministry of some kind, or simply because they are fascinated by the subject. This does not necessarily presuppose that Christian faith is considered more important or truer to reality than other kinds of theology. Whether or not there are reasons to defend such a position will be a part of the discussion.

Christian faith has a specific content, builds upon certain presuppositions, and is founded on particular sources. What I primarily want to discuss in this book, is the relation between the content of the faith and the methods one uses to study, appropriate, and communicate it. All academic disciplines have a debate concerning which methods and sources are most relevant in relation to its specific field of study. Which methods and which sources are the most relevant for working with God, divine revelation, and the believers' God-relationship? These are the main topics of this book.

The relation between content and method is as important in theology as in other academic disciplines. If theology does not maintain a consistent relationship between content and method, theological work will distort its object more than it explicates it. One will then simply have taken a set of presuppositions according to one's own liking and applied them arbitrarily on the understanding on the God-relationship. When this occurs, a wedge is inserted between the study of theology and the life in the church, the outcome of which is that by studying theology one becomes less, not more, prepared for church service. In addition, one will have lost the possibility of the widening of perspective that follows from working on the Christian faith from its own presuppositions.

Which questions are the most important to ask when we want to get a principled and well-argued understanding of the relationship between content and method in Christian theology? A natural place to start is in the current debate on the understanding of knowledge. At least for the last hundred years, there has been a lively debate in the area of research that is commonly called philosophy of science. What are the implications of this debate for the self-understanding of theology as an academic discipline? What are the criteria for accepting something as knowledge, and are these criteria something theology can and should strive to satisfy (chapter 2)?

Theology works with the understanding of God. A natural next step will then be to look at the main aspects of the Christian view of God and investigate its possible methodological implications. The first thing that is said about God both in the Bible and in the main Christian creeds is that *God has created the world*. This implies that the Christian faith, and all other faiths with a similar understanding of God, have a specific understanding of the relationship between God and everything else. God is Creator and everything else is created. What does this mean, and what are the implications of this distinction for our understanding of theological method? A discussion of this question must take place in dialogue with those who think that we have no reason to believe in a Creator at all. This is also a theological position in the sense that it gives an answer to one of the most important questions in theology (chapter 3).

If what we say about God is to be considered trustworthy, it must somehow reflect God's own reality. This presupposes that the Creator has uncovered (revealed) something about himself[3] within the framework of the created, and that he has done in such a way that we in a methodologically consistent way can work with the notion of humans as receivers and mediators of divine revelation. All revelation-based theologies agree on this point. However, Christian theology takes one important further step, declaring that the most important revelation occurred when God became a human being. What is the implication of the incarnation for the understanding of Christian theology? And how should Christian theology relate to theologies that maintain a doctrine of divine revelation but reject the idea of divine incarnation (chapter 4)?

In addition, Christian theology maintains that the goal of God's self-disclosure is to include humans in a believing fellowship. A bridge is constructed between the Creator and the created in such a way that it governs our understanding of doctrine and life. How are we included in this fellowship, and what are the implications for the understanding of theology from our way of answering this question? Some theologians think that the God-relationship is the outcome of a free and conscious choice by an independent individual who has carefully considered all options. Others think that a faith relationship is the result of finding oneself at the receiving end of God's creative communication. These two approaches give quite different,

---

3. I follow the biblical practice of referring to God with the pronoun in the masculine without presupposing that God is gendered. The question is discussed more in detail in what follows.

and probably mutually exclusive, understandings of theological method. The question of how faith is established and nourished is thus a question with crucial implications for theology's understanding of itself (chapter 5).

The first part of the book will in this way investigate theology's self-understanding by discussing creation, revelation, and anthropology as methodological challenges. After having cleared the ground in this way, the second part of the book will consider the sources of the Christian faith, how to work with them, and the mutual relationship between them. Traditionally, Christian theology works with four different kinds of sources: The Bible, the tradition of the church, experience, and reason. How can we work with these sources as both an intellectual, a spiritual, and an existential challenge in such a way that we are included in the reality manifested through the revelation (chapters 6 through 9).

In the final chapter I will summarize the main findings of the book and discuss their implication for the practice of studying theology, whether the reader is a full-time student of theology or not. How should we work with theology so that we can appropriate its content in a good way?

I have tried to write this book such that the only requirement for benefitting from it is an interest in the topics discussed. I have therefore explained terminology and tried to write as simply as possible. But there is always a certain level beyond which problems cannot be simplified without disappearing. Some readers may therefore find some passages and chapters to be quite demanding. It helps if one has some knowledge of the Bible and the history of theology in advance. Some familiarity with the current debate on philosophy of science and the history of philosophy and science will also be helpful. There are lots of handbooks available that give the necessary background information.[4]

The relation between theology and its contemporary context is an important topic. One should therefore study theology—and this book—with a view to contemporary culture. From where in contemporary culture can theology find impulses for its task of conveying divine revelation, and which elements in contemporary culture will theology have to criticize to maintain its own integrity? I will give some suggestions for answering questions like these, but the most important work in this respect must be done by the individual readers.

---

4. See, e.g., Okasha, *Philosophy of Science: A Very Short Introduction*; Hägglund, *History of Theology*; McGrath, *Historical Theology*; Warburton, *A Little History of Philosophy*; McGrath, *Christian Theology: An Introduction*.

The goal of the book is that after having read it one should have a better understanding of theology in its academic context. In this way, one should be better equipped to work with concrete questions related to the interpretation of the Bible, church history, systematic and practical theology in a way that is both constructive and has self-critical awareness. The study of these disciplines is, however, not the topic of this book.

FIRST PART

Theology as an academic discipline

2

The question of theological knowledge

Knowledge, truth, and justification

WHAT DOES IT MEAN to know, and how is knowledge established? In some cases, questions like these are easily answered. One can look up the table of contents to find the number of chapters in this book. Other phenomena, like gravitation or love, are more complicated, but they are to some extent knowable by studying the mutual relations between observable phenomena. The relation to God is different, because it cannot be taken for granted that God is part of the observable world. How can knowledge about God then be justified?

To answer this question, we must first clarify what it is to know something. Knowledge is often defined as "justified true belief."[1] What distinguishes knowledge from mere belief is that knowledge is justified. We can think that something is the case, and this can be true or untrue. However, when we add a justification, the statement is raised from the level of opinion to the level of knowledge. I can presume that a certain student has some knowledge of epistemology. Then I get to read this student's exam essay, where the understanding of knowledge in contemporary philosophy is explained in detail, and I know (on the condition that there has been no cheating) that this student is indeed well-informed in the topic of epistemology.

What, then, are the requirements of a good justification? This is not always as straightforward as in the example of the student. And what do we mean when we say that something is true? There is a lot of discussion about this, and we will therefore have to look more closely at these questions.

---

1. Ichikawa and Steup, *The Analysis of Knowledge*.

Truth is a concept that can be understood in different ways.[2] We can think that something is true because it works. Explanations in natural science are true because they let us manipulate nature in useful ways. We can make computers and airplanes, and they work. This is called a *pragmatic understanding of truth*. However, we are usually more philosophically ambitious than that. Basically, we think a statement is true because it tells us what is the case. A person is said to be a hardworking student if this person works with the required reading and always comes well prepared to lectures. The theory of gravity is true because it correctly describes the physical relation between bodies. A statement is true when it corresponds to reality. This is called the *correspondence theory of truth*.

This can seem to be too obvious to be questioned. This is the test we use to distinguish between truth and lie both in everyday life and in more formal contexts, e.g., in court. Did I attend the lecture today, or was I relaxing in the cantina? We usually do not need advanced investigations to find the answer to that question. Is the prosecuting attorney's claim that the accused was at the scene of the crime and put the knife in the victim true or not? Either the accused has done this, and then the claim is true, or the accused has not done it, and then the claim is false. As long as we proceed according to the correspondence theory of truth, it does not get more complicated than that.

However, it is not always easy to establish an unambiguous link between statement and reality. There are different reasons for that. Verbal statements and non-verbal entities are different aspects of reality, and it is not obvious that it is possible to defend the existence of a direct link between them without presupposing it. On a more practical level, we may have to struggle with the existence of conflicting statements about the same reality. Some person claims to have seen the accused at the scene of the crime, while another provides an alibi. Or we may be interested in phenomena that are unobservable, either because they belong to the past, or because direct observations are impossible for other reasons. To the last group belong both physical phenomena, e.g., in the nucleus of the atom, or abstract phenomena like justice and love. In these cases, we must put together different observations and interpret them to be able to make statements about the atomic nucleus, justice, and love. Does that imply that the truth value of these statements is undecidable? Following the demands of a strict correspondence theory, this seems to be the case, but is that something we would want to maintain?

2. Glanzberg, *Truth*.

Several thinkers have therefore tried to avoid the dilemmas of a strict correspondence theory by replacing or supplementing it with a so-called coherence theory. What is supposed to cohere according to this theory are different statements concerning the phenomenon under investigation. One abandons the ambition of creating an unambiguous correspondence between statement and non-verbal reality and is content with the demand that a true statement should cohere with other true and relevant statements. This is a view of truth that is easily applicable both theoretically and practically. One does not need a (philosophically ambitious) theory of the relation between verbal statements and non-verbal realities, and we create a room for working scientifically and academically with phenomena that cannot be confirmed by simple and unambiguous observations.

Historical sciences work in this way when they investigate what different sources can say about a certain phenomenon, and when they see these sources together, they establish a justified account of what occurred. Claims about what Martin Luther said and did at the Diet in Worms in 1521 cannot build on either video recordings or interviews with eyewitnesses, but we have quite detailed reports on what he said, and scholars therefore think they can give a fairly precise account of what really happened. Legal courts work in this way then they compare and evaluate statements from witnesses and other kinds of relevant proof material to find what really happened. Natural science establishes theories by interpreting relevant aspects of a phenomenon without necessarily claiming to be able to observe the phenomenon directly. In this way, we have got advanced theories about what happens in atomic nuclei while being aware that they will never be directly observable. There are also many who think that statements concerning justice and injustice can be true or untrue, even if that requires that the phenomena that are investigated be placed in an interpretative framework.

This does not imply that the correspondence theory is wrong. That I now am writing this book, is true because that is what I am doing. However, it is insufficient, because statements may have the property of truth even if the correspondence theory is too crude to allow for this conclusion. It must therefore be completed by a coherence theory, which claims that a statement is true when it coheres with other true statements. This is often what occurs both in everyday life, in legal courts, and in scholarly and scientific investigations.

However, even the coherence theory cannot stand alone. The history of science gives us many examples of great theories that have seem to be quite coherent but in fact are wrong. Through most of human history, it was an accepted truth that the sun, the planets, and the stars move around the earth. What we observe every day is easily interpreted this way, and the model can be used for precise astronomic theories and true predictions of astronomic phenomena like eclipses and planetary conjunctions. It is thus highly coherent but does not correspond to the fact that neither the earth nor any other point in the universe is an absolute point of orientation for the movements of stars and planets. Something similar can be said about Newtonian physics as the summary of what we call the scientific revolution. Newtonian physics is a comprehensive theory of the relation between power, mass, velocity, and acceleration for all physical objects in the universe, and it describes everything precisely if velocities are small in relation to the speed of light. But it does not agree with the fact that the speed of light is a constant. Newtonian physics is coherent but untrue.

My point of departure for this discussion of the understanding of truth was the definition of knowledge as justified, true belief. What we have found so far is that truth is something that is not easily defined. The meaning of something being true cannot be put in a simple formula. A true statement should correspond to reality, but to test whether this is the case or not can only be done in specific cases, and then not in a philosophically precise way. We therefore often test the truth value of statements by means of other statements. However, there are situations where testing in relation to non-verbal reality will be highly relevant. It may not be possible to advance much beyond this conclusion.

What, then, are the criteria for good justifications? This must have something to do with statements' testability. Scholarly work is done in such a way that general statements are established from simple observations. These general statements are called hypotheses. They may be statements concerning something that occurs repeatedly and regularly (that is often the case in natural science), or statements concerning the nature of a particular situation (that is often the case in historical disciplines). Hypotheses are established by inductions, which are inferences from the observed to the unobserved or to general laws. There are no exact rules for inductions; any given phenomenon or historical process can always be explained in different ways. Inductions are therefore never final and definitive because the possibility of the discovery of counterexamples can never be excluded. One may make new and unexpected observations (cf. the unforeseen discovery that speed of light was a constant independent of the relative speed of the source of light). Or a scholar may discover unknown sources that let certain historical events appear in a new light. Induction is a kind of intelligent guesswork. This is a fundamental and unalterable condition for all kinds of scholarly and scientific work.

Hypotheses must therefore be tested. This is done by means of deduction, which differs from induction in the sense that deductions always follow from the premises as a matter of logical necessity. The hypothesis to be tested is typically taken as one of premises of the argument, and one then deduces what will happen in a particular situation if the hypothesis is true. If Newton's law of gravitation is correct, all falling bodies will fall in a specific way. This can be computed in advance for all particular cases and then measured in order to test the hypothesis.

The rules of deductions are investigated in the subject we call logic, which tells us what the criteria for valid and sound arguments are. Arguments are said to be valid if there are no errors in the argumentative structure. If the premises of the argument are true, a valid argument is also a sound argument. All sound arguments are valid, but not all valid arguments are sound, because premises may be untrue. To give an example: If all students are left-handed, then all philosophy students are lefthanded. This is a valid argument, but it is not sound, because the premise is untrue; not all students are left-handed.

For our purpose here, we do not need to go further into the intricacies of logical analysis. It is more interesting to look at the criteria for the evaluation of hypotheses. In the 1920s there was a school in the philosophy of science called logical positivism that said that statements can only be evaluated in a meaningful way if they can be confirmed by repeatable observations. What does not strictly follow from repeatable observations does not make sense according to this school of thought. The important thing is therefore to develop hypotheses that can be tested empirically. The law of gravity predicts the time necessary for falling objects to travel the distance from A to B, and these predictions are easily testable. Therefore, the law of gravity is a scientifically meaningful statement. Hypotheses that cannot be tested by sense experience in this way, the logical positivists considered meaningless. They thus did not only recommend verification or confirmation of hypotheses through sense experience but insisted that statements that could not be tested in this way, did not make sense. Well-established academic disciplines like history and literature studies were therefore not seen as meaningful activities by the logical positivists.

However, there are several problems with this theory. For one thing, the statement that all statements must be empirically verifiable is not itself empirically verifiable; the theory does not fulfil its own requirement. Another problem is the status of logical and mathematical statements (2+2=4). Are such statements true because they are empirically verifiable? If that is not the case, are they then meaningless? And what about the status of inductive generalizations? Consider the statement "all metals expand when heated." This is a statement that can never be fully justified experimentally (we can never test all possible cases of heating of all metals), but does that make it meaningless?

The philosopher of science Karl R. Popper (1902–94) therefore in the 1930s suggested replacing the criterion of verification with a criterion of falsification.[3] In his view, the most important issue for testing a hypothesis was not to check whether it was empirically verifiable. The crucial thing was to check whether it could be empirically *falsified*. If one succeeds in falsifying a theory, one has actually learned something—that the hypothesis is wrong—while verification at its worst confirms false prejudice. The demand for falsification even has another advantage; it forces us to formulate the hypothesis as inclusively and precisely as possible. A vague hypothesis can almost always be confirmed (good students receive better marks than bad students), but in order to be falsified, the hypothesis must be precise and ambitious (students who work x hours every week will with y percent probability get at least a C). Working with a verification criterion, one may therefore inadvertently express one's hypothesis quite vaguely. The falsification criterion forces us to be more ambitious. We must be able to indicate precisely the conditions under which the hypothesis is true. It was the demand for precision that led to Newtonian physics being replaced by Einsteinian relativity. Light emitted from moving objects did not behave as predicted by the Newtonian model. Therefore, the Newtonian model could not be correct.

Popper's theory is called critical rationalism and was a clear advance over logical positivism. He made it into a scholarly ideal to write as precisely and accurately as possible, and he was skeptical of comprehensive theories that did not take the possibility of falsification seriously. In this way, he tried to distinguish between the undoubtedly acceptable and the more dubious without being as rigorous as the logical positivists. He was

---

3. Popper, *The Logic of Scientific Discovery*. Originally published in German in 1934; the first English translation appeared in 1959.

even critical of theories in medicine and natural science. He considered Freud's psychoanalysis with suspicion, as it seems to explain all kinds of behavior by referring to traumatic experiences during childhood. In a similar way he was critical of Darwinian evolution theory, as this is a theory that tends to explain everything by the principle of the survival of the fittest. In his view, they are examples of theories that try to explain everything without establishing testable criteria for falsification. In Popper's view, they should say that if such and such phenomenon occurs, the theory is falsified, but they do the opposite: They explain both a certain phenomenon and its opposite with the same theory. Freud does not change his theory even if persons with traumatic childhood experience turn out to be quite normal as adults. Darwin does not specify observations that might disprove his theory. There were therefore in Popper's view unsatisfactory as scientific theories.

On the other hand, critical rationalism is not quite as critical towards the historical disciplines as logical positivism had been. It is not in principle impossible to establish falsifiable theories about the past and test them on the available sources. Neither is it essential that falsification is immediately testable in a simple way. E.g., we may have to wait for a specific astronomical phenomenon to occur to be able to check a certain physical hypothesis. Popper's falsification criterion merely says that one must be able to establish a concrete prediction that in principle can be found to be true or untrue.

Popper furnishes us with many good points and observations. His contention that one should write as ambitiously and precisely as the sources allows, is certainly good advice for all kinds of academic writing. However, there is one phenomenon that is not well integrated in his thought. One should indeed look for possible ways to falsify claims. Experience tells us, though, that one (or a few) surprising observations will not result in the abandonment of a well-established theory. Other strategies will always be tried before considering abandonment. One will either deny the confusing observation or try to incorporate it into the prevailing theory by means of so-called ad hoc hypotheses, which say that for some reason, what usually happens does not happen in this case. The theory that the disputed observation is supposed to falsify will not be written off as entirely wrong on the basis of a few anomalous pieces of data; it will still explain quite a lot. It will thus only be partially falsified. The problem is that nobody knows which part is wrong.[4]

---

4. Stanford, *Underdetermination for Scientific Theory*.

This was the point of the departure for the probably most well-known and discussed approach to philosophy of science in the twentieth century, Thomas Kuhn's (1922–96) book *The Structure of Scientific Revolutions* from 1962. Differing from both logical positivism and critical rationalism, Kuhn does not want to define what science should be. He works empirically and tries to explain how science works.

First, he describes what he calls normal science. This is what goes on within an academic fellowship where everybody agrees what the main problems and the main concepts are, and where there is a well-established tradition for which sources one should investigate and which methods one should use. Research aims at producing new knowledge based on these common presuppositions, which are not supposed to be challenged. In medicine, one does research on new drugs and new surgical techniques without anybody questioning the principles according to which research is conducted. Astronomy explores the surface of Saturn or the physics of distant galaxies without questioning the accepted cosmology or prevailing methodology. "Paradigms" is what Kuhn calls these established models for understanding and research.

However, from time to time somebody makes observations that seem to question elements of the established paradigm. One famous example from the history of science is that planets move in ways that differ from what should be expected from the geocentric worldview—that is the reason they are called planets (wandering star, from Greek *planáō*, to wander; they seem to wander among the other stars). Another example is that light behaves differently from what should be expected from a Newtonian model of the universe (the speed of light is a constant irrespective of the relative speed of the light source). These observations did not lead to the immediate abolishment of the established theory but to the theory being modified by ad hoc hypotheses. This situation can last for a long time; with the geocentric worldview, it lasted several thousand years. Then it might happen that somebody takes the problematic observation as the point of departure for a new understanding of this particular branch of learning and its methods. This "somebody" will regularly be found in the periphery of the guild of scholars. This is exemplified both by Copernicus, who first suggested the hypothesis of a heliocentric worldview, and by Albert Einstein, who suggested that Newtonian physics should be replaced by the theory of relativity. The established professors have their careers invested in the paradigm under attack and will therefore be inclined to defend it. If the new suggestion is sufficiently strong, meaning that it explains everything the old paradigm explains and then some more without ad hoc hypotheses, we will have a struggle between the defenders of the old and the new paradigms.

Kuhn calls this struggle between paradigms a scientific crisis. A crisis is a scholarly debate that is not concerned with the interpretation of a specific observation but with the identity and self-understanding of the subject of the debating scholars. The fundamental presuppositions of their scholarly work are challenged. This struggle can be both tough and lengthy, and other factors than the strictly academic, like academic reputation and sources of income for scholars and institutions, are always involved.

The outcome of the struggle will not always be a clear conclusion. We then have to live with a situation where there is more than one paradigm in play. Normally, however, one of the competing paradigms will be the victor. It will then replace the old one as the framework of a new way of doing normal science. The scientific revolution has succeeded. Further along the road, one may discover new anomalies that will result in a new crisis. In Kuhn's view, ground-breaking scientific innovations always occur in this way. A fundamental reorientation, reconfiguring the commonly accepted presuppositions of an area of research, will never take place without struggle.

An important part of the self-understanding of what Kuhn calls normal science are the criteria for truth. A scientific crisis is therefore not only a discussion of the truth of a specific hypothesis; it is a discussion of what it means for something to be true. Should a theory in natural science be confirmed by everyday experience? This was Aristotle's position. In that case, both the heliocentric cosmology and the theory of relativity have problems defending themselves. Neither is confirmed by our immediate experience, as both for their confirmation dependent are on specialized observations and advanced technological equipment. Should a theory of natural science give us a consistent and uniform worldview? For almost a century, modern physics has struggled without success to unify relativity and quantum mechanics. Still, its models are considered to be a significant advancement beyond Newton's physics, even if his model does not have this ambiguity.

Kuhn's point in this context is that there is no absolute and universal criterion for truth. The criteria for what is considered to be true change with the paradigm within which one is working. This is another confirmation of the significance of the understanding of truth as coherence. Within a paradigm, statements and models are supposed to cohere. On the other hand, the importance of unexpected observations confirms the significance of the understanding of truth as correspondence. It is the experience that there is something fundamental that does not fit that makes the old paradigm crumble and to be replaced by another one.

The affinity between Kuhn's understanding of scientific revolutions and a coherence-based understanding of truth has led some scholars to criticize Kuhn for have a relativistic understanding of knowledge. If everything is reduced to a never-ending battle between paradigms, we will never know what is true. However, the fact that ultimate truth may be unattainable does not imply that all statements are equal as far as their truth value is concerned. For a theory to count as a scientific paradigm, there are certain requirements that must be met. A scientific paradigm must be able to explain all known phenomena and be a fruitful starting point for further research. Newton's gravitation equations are correct for all phenomena with a relatively slow speed, but they are not the ultimate truth about gravity (which is still to be discovered). It is perfectly acceptable to say about a dictatorial tyrant that this person is unjust without pretending to know everything about justice. It is possible to say about that something is true without having to proclaim that we have found the ultimate truth about the world. We probably never will. But along our way towards this goal, we may discover lesser truths that are both interesting and relevant. This is not new knowledge; this is the understanding of truth that is found already in Plato's dialogues.[5]

We must be able to formulate what we think we know as true and justified statements. The justified, true belief account is a robust definition, even if it seems to be impossible to find definitions of truth and justification that are universally applicable. Precise and universally valid criteria for justified knowledge are elusive. This situation does not leave us in complete darkness. Not everything we think we know is erroneous and misleading. At least some of it seems to be both reasonable and relevant. However, it is provisional and always in need of improvement. We will probably have new scientific revolutions, which will alter established academic subjects in radical and unexpected ways. We have no reason to believe that we have reached the final goal as far as knowledge of the world is concerned. More important than knowledge as a set of final propositions is therefore the investigation of how knowledge is developed, appropriated, and improved.

---

5. Gerson, *Ancient Epistemology*, 38.

Method is important. This is true for all subjects. The most important requirement is openness as far as presuppositions and justifications are concerned. Statements that demand that parts of their justification are shielded from critique do not meet the basic requirements for scholarly work. The same is true for statements that are obviously wrong or have inconsistent justifications. We may not always agree on the application of these criteria. They are still important, though, as the starting points for the discussion. We must always be open to the possibility that established knowledge may be partly untrue. This should stimulate creativity and thinking outside the preestablished patters. Radically new knowledge is always developed in this way.

What, then, are the implications of these general reflections on the theory of science for the understanding of theology as an academic subject?

Theological knowledge

When the European universities were established in medieval times, they had four faculties: theology, philosophy, law, and medicine. Theology and philosophy were the most important ones, as the most comprehensive questions were asked here. Can theology, then, comply with the understanding of knowledge as justified true belief? In medieval times, one thought it could. Then it was rather a question whether the other academic subjects could satisfy the definition. Now the tables have been turned. Today, many think that theology does not satisfy the definition of knowledge as justified true belief, and that theology therefore should be relegated from the university. If we accept logical positivism and a one-sided correspondence theory of truth, this is a natural conclusion. Statements about God and about humans' relationship with God are not founded on simple and straightforward reports of repeatable observations. Does this imply that theology is a speculative and unfounded form of scholarly work?

The problem with this critique, however, is that neither logical positivism nor a one-sided correspondence theory is an acceptable theory. They work with criteria for truth they do not themselves satisfy. In addition, their critique does not apply only to theology, but to all knowledge concerning past and/or non-repeatable phenomena. There are few who today would maintain that the past and the non-repeatable are uninteresting areas of research.

Critical rationalism is quite different in this respect. Popper's demand that academically interesting statements should be as ambitious and precise as sources allow are not more problematic for theology than for other subjects studying the work of humans, and a demand that should be accepted by everybody. Vague statements with unclear justifications are as uninteresting in theology as any other academic discipline. This is true for all levels, from simple student assignments to advanced scholarly work.

What, then, about the criterion of falsifiability? Is this something theology should accept? Theology continually works with historical sources, and therefore makes statements concerning how to understand these sources. These statements should be evaluated as similar statements on other historically oriented areas of research. The discussion concerning the applicability of the criterion of falsifiability for these subjects will thus be directly relevant also for theology.

However, theology does not only work with historical statements but makes statements concerning God as the frame and origin of reality. Is the criterion of falsifiability applicable even to this kind of statements?

The British philosopher Antony Flew (1923–2010) thought that the criterion of falsifiability could not be satisfied as far as statements concerning God is concerned, and that theology for that reason could not be accepted as science.[6] Popper thought that Darwin and Freud interpreted all phenomena according to a simple principle that was modified as needed without ever being falsified. He therefore dismissed their work as unscientific. In a similar way, Flew understood theological statements as comprehensive assertions that could never be checked through precise, falsifiable observations. The idea of a non-material, never directly observable Creator was understood by Flew to invite an endless series of modifications of the original idea which never asked the decisive question: Does this shadowy figure really exist? A theological system of statements may be internally coherent, but it does not have any purchase on reality because it refuses to allow itself to be falsified.

The German theologian Wolfhart Pannenberg (1928–2014) took Popper's challenge seriously and thought that theology should aim at satisfying the criterion of falsifiability.[7] In this way one could avoid the kind of critique

---

6. Flew, *Theology and Falsification* (originally a paper presented in the Socratic Club in Oxford, presided over by C. S. Lewis).

7. Pannenberg, *Theology and the Philosophy of Science*; Murphy, *Theology in the Age of Scientific Reasoning*, chapter 2.

presented by Flew. Pannenberg thought that theological knowledge should be understood as a historically argued statement concerning how God as the Lord of history would let history end. Some historical events are more interesting than others because they are easily interpreted as anticipations of the end of history. Here Pannenberg is thinking of the life, death, and resurrection of Jesus, which according to the Christian faith are interpreted as a prediction that Jesus by the end of time "will come again in glory to judge the living and the dead" (Nicene Creed).[8] This is in principle a falsifiable statement; when history eventually ends, the statement will be proved or disproved depending on what actually occurs. The statement cannot be checked immediately, but this is the case even in other areas of research without their status as sciences being questioned. The point is that the statement gives us falsifiable information. By focusing on this, Pannenberg thought he could show that theology satisfied the general demands for something to be considered as scientific.

Pannenberg has been met with critique, partly because the principle of falsifiability itself has been criticized, partly because its application in a theological context makes theology into a testable scientific hypothesis. Is this an adequate way of understanding faith in God? Believers within the monotheistic traditions of belief usually understand God as absolute and non-negotiable. They do not think of God as something that is real or not pending the outcome of some future event. Is this an approach that might be integrated in Pannenberg's perspective? If not, Pannenberg's own project might be as problematic as the one he seeks to replace, as it then appears as a distortion of the phenomenon it studies. Is the criterion of falsifiability at all compatible with the character of faith as maintained in its classical sources? If not, the interesting question is whether one, by taking the understanding of faith in these sources as one's point of departure, can reject the criterion of falsifiability without being subject to Flew's critique. Pannenberg's attempt at developing a theological theory of science does not address this question. He redefines the question according to his own understanding of faith before answering it, and that is a methodologically dubious procedure.[9]

Kuhn's approach is more easily applicable in a theological context. The demand for openness and reliability concerning presuppositions, sources, methods, and arguments is unproblematic, and is confirmed by the Bible's

---

8. Quoted from Kolb and Wengert, *The Book of Concord*, 23.
9. Brink, *Philosophy of Science for Theologians*, 176–81.

emphasis on the significance of truth. Neither does theology have any problems with the statement that the understanding of truth is anchored in a specific worldview ("paradigm"). "I am . . . the truth," Jesus says (John 14:6), and he claims that "if anyone's will is to do God's will, he will know" whether the teachings of Jesus are reliable or not (John 7:17). Truth is thus, even in the Bible, connected with practice in a specific context.

The history of theology also confirms Kuhn's understanding of scientific crises and the significance of paradigm changes. The most important paradigm change in Christian theology occurred with the change in the understanding of the Bible and of reality that was included in the conviction that Jesus was the promised Messiah. This paradigm change is still disputed. Judaism still reads what the Christians call the Old Testament from the presupposition that Jesus was not the promised Messiah. A similar paradigm change, though not quite as profound as the former one, occurred when late medieval scholasticism was replaced by the differently oriented understanding of knowledge and reality in the Reformation. One of Martin Luther's (1483-1546) first actions as a reformer was to revise the program for the study of theology at the University in Wittenberg according to the new theological paradigm, which allegedly was closer to the paradigm of the early church than what had been the case in scholasticism. It is still disputed whether this was a correct assessment or not, though the adherents of both paradigms are nowadays not as antagonistic as they used to be.

However, if theology accepts Kuhn's understanding of science, it must also consider the critique that Kuhn relativizes the understanding of truth. If truth[10] is intricately connected to practice in a specific context, can it still be universally valid? The cosmology of modern physics was established in a certain context with specific presuppositions. Can it then claim to present a universally valid knowledge of the real structures of the world? This question is paralleled by the question whether theological knowledge anchored in a specific tradition of mediating divine revelation can justifiably claim to transmit universally relevant knowledge.

On Kuhn's understanding, the contextual situatedness of truth is a problem that affects all academic subjects. All have ambitions of producing true knowledge established within the context of a specific paradigm. This is not a situation that is unique for theology. However, theology has the advantage of always having been aware of the problem. Already the Old

---

10 By "truth" here, I mean both (a) the things that we consider to be true and (b) the meaning of the word "truth."

Testament prophets reflect on their finding themselves within the context of a specific tradition while proclaiming a universally valid truth (cf. Isa 44:8). The awareness of this tension has followed Christian theology until today and should never disappear. If it does, theology will deteriorate to the conservation of specific traditions unable to pose critical and constructive questions to its own self-understanding. There is thus no opposition between the demands of the philosophy of science and the self-understanding of theology in this respect. Theology will always have to discuss the tension between the contingence of contextuality and the ambition of proclaiming a universal truth, and has a long tradition of doing just that.

There thus seems to be nothing in the contemporary debate on philosophy of science that should indicate that theology does not satisfy the commonly accepted criteria for the production and transmission of knowledge. Some have tried to define these criteria in such a way that theology was excluded, but this attempt has been largely abandoned. What remains to be discussed, however, is whether the general criteria for what can be accepted as knowledge can be justified when God is the alleged source for the knowledge one seeks to establish. Does this imply that (parts of) the knowledge theology claims to be working with is exempt from the principle of falsification? If that is the case, we will have to ask whether it is possible to limit the criterion of falsifiability without committing the error of inducing "death by a thousand qualifications" (Flew's critique). This will be the main topic of chapter 3. In addition, we need to discuss the relation between contextuality and universality concerning the truth claims of theology. If theology is understood as reflection on revelation given to a specific group of people in a particular context, what is the justification for claiming that theology produces universal knowledge? Is it possible to maintain in a trustworthy and reliable way that the God who is presented as the Creator of heaven and earth has revealed himself by becoming a human being at a particular place and time in human history? This will be the central topic of chapter 4.

3

What does it mean that the world is created?

God's unknowability

THE FIRST STATEMENT IN the Bible is the claim that God has created heaven and earth, in other words, everything that exists (Gen 1:1). In this way there is established a fundamental distinction between God and everything else. God is Creator, while all else is created and is not God. The most important thing one from this starting point can say about God is that God is no part of the world in which we, with all our experiences, thoughts, and reflections, are situated. What is the significance of this observation for our way of working with theological questions?

Let us first look at the way the biblical authors approach this problem. The distinction between God and the world is something they return to and unfolds in different contexts. Among them is the question of how we as thinking and believing humans relate to God. The revelation of the law of God maintains the distinction between God and the world by explicitly prohibiting the making of images of God by copying anything in the world (Exod 20:4). Confusing Creator and creation with the outcome that one worships elements of the created in the belief that it is God, is an offence against the first commandment and thus the most serious and fundamental of all sins (Isa 45:20; Ps 115:4–8; Rom 1:25). Many times, in both the Old and the New Testament, it is emphasized that nobody can see, or has ever seen God (Exod 33:20; John 1:18a). God cannot be experienced directly. This is expressed in figural language using metaphors of both light and darkness. God is hidden by an impenetrable darkness (Pss 18:9; 97:2) and "dwells in unapproachable light" (1 Tim 6:16). It can also be expressed more directly. In the Old Testament, we have statements concerning the difference and immeasurability of God (Isa 55:8–9; Job 11:7–9). In the New Testament, we have more principled statements about God's unknowability and inscrutability (Rom 11:33).

This understanding of the world as dependent on an origin beyond its limits, is universally accessible. It may be established through reflection on the mystery of the existence of the world (Job 12:7–10; Rom 1:19–20). However, because one is not always conscious of the problem for theological thought that is created by God being located outside or beyond the world within which believers exist, humans are indeed inclined to make their own images of God. While not directly transgressing the first commandment by making physical images, one can still err by making images in one's *mind*. Humans' reflection on the Origin of the world (i.e., God) therefore tend to consist of an appropriate appreciation of the *difference* of the Origin from the creation, enlarged by one's own ideas and reflections on how it presumably behaves. Though even in this way—by creating mental images of God—one may violate the prohibition against idolatry.

The Bible was written in a context where the prohibition against idolatry was taken seriously in theory, though not always in practice. When the early Christian church made its first tentative steps outside the Jewish context, where the prohibition of idolatry was generally accepted, it found itself within the Hellenistic context, where the relation to the problem of idolatry was considerably more relaxed. The prevailing myths presented the gods with human-like characteristics without anybody considering this a problem. The strict biblical distinction between Creator and creation was not appreciated. When presenting a Christian worldview within this context, the question of how to relate to the biblical prohibition of idolatry immediately became a central one.

Both Jews and Christian found a philosophical ally in the tradition of Platonism. Socrates was condemned to death because he allegedly had expressed critique against the Greek, polytheistic myths. This contributed to the understanding of Socrates as a kind of pre-Christian saint. In addition, in the Platonic tradition the church fathers found an advanced reflection on God's difference and unknowability. In *Republic*, Plato had written about the sun as being both inaccessible and unknowable for us. We cannot explore the sun by gazing at it; we will only be blinded by its light. Still, it is the light from the sun that lets everything else appear as knowable and explorable. In a similar way, our (moral) knowledge is established through the light of a source that in itself is inaccessible.[1] Both the image and its implication are quite close to what is found in the New Testament: God is light; let us therefore walk in the light (1 John 1:5–7), even though we have no direct access to the light itself. Later thinkers within the Platonic tradition, notably Plotinus in the second century AD and Proclus in the fourth, interpreted the Platonic approach theologically as a doctrine of the unknowable One that is the origin of everything else. The Neoplatonism of Plotinus and Proclus is thus a kind of philosophical religiosity.[2]

Philo, a Jew who lived in Alexandria in Egypt and was a contemporary of the events of the New Testament, referred to this philosophical tradition when explaining central elements in the biblical understanding of God. Following his example, the church fathers used the same tradition as an important dialogue partner both when clarifying for themselves and other Christians how they should understand the biblical principle of divine unknowability and when explaining the Christian understanding of God as Creator to people unfamiliar with the Jewish rejection of idolatry.

This union of the biblical understanding of God and Greek philosophy presented itself quite easily for Christians as Paul had made use of the same kind of argument. On his mission travels, he even came to Athens. There he made a speech on the Areopagus, commenting on the altar for the unknown God he had found in the city (Acts 17:23). This kind of belief among people who do not know God's revelation is something Paul considers as exemplary. They know there is a God, but they also know that their knowledge of God is quite limited, and they therefore content themselves with worshipping the Unknown. Thus, Paul suggests that it may be possible to develop a natural, reason-based understanding of God that refrains from making the arbitrary and unfounded move to idolatry. It remains void of content in respect of the God of whom one has a presentiment, but who still has not made himself known. So, it may be possible to maintain a consistent worship without identifying God arbitrarily with elements of the created world.

In this way, there was created an alliance between a biblical faith in God and elements of Greek philosophy, and this alliance created the context within which Christian thinking developed. The alliance became particularly important in the Greek part of Christendom, and the thought of the Orthodox Church is to this day deeply influenced by this approach.

1. Plato, *Republic* 507b–509c.
2. Alfsvåg, *What No Mind Has Conceived*, 21–31

WHAT DOES IT MEAN THAT THE WORLD IS CREATED?

The most important of the church fathers in the Western, Latin part of Christendom, Augustine (354–430), was also influenced by the dialogue with Platonism, and through him, this way of thinking therefore became essential also in Western Europe.[3]

The Greek-Christian philosophical tradition understood itself as reflection on the conditions of human understanding given with the appropriation of the idea of the unknown Origin of the world. For this Origin, the limitations that are relevant for all other phenomena do not apply. Differing from everything outside itself, the Origin of the world is *infinite* and *unlimited*. That is the reason it is *unknowable*, as knowability presupposes the existence of defining limits of what is known. The word "definition" is derived from the Latin word *finis*, meaning limit. To define something, is to set its limits, but this is a procedure that *cannot* be applied to God as infinite and eternal. However, since all that exists has its origin in God, indefinability also in a derived sense pertains to the created. Even events and phenomena in the created world thus retain an element of unknowability; they will never be fully understood. Our understanding is adequate only to the extent that we know that we do not fully understand. This primarily pertains to our understanding of God, but even affects the created. This kind of epistemology, which defined Christian thinking until the thirteenth century, is called apophatic or negative theology (from Greek *apóphasis* = negation), because it is concerned with the fact that our concepts and ideas concerning God never fully grasp the reality. They will therefore in some sense always have to be negated before they can be used.[4]

Paul has good ways of expressing this limited ability of the human intellect both in relation to God and the world. In his well-known passage on (divine) love he wrote that we "see in a glass, darkly" (1 Cor 13:12; KJV). Earlier in the same letter he expresses the limitations set by a biblical epistemology in the following interesting way: "If anyone imagines that he knows something, he does not yet know as he ought to know" (8:2). Knowledge is only adequate when we understand that we still have not fully understood. In its original context, this quotation is part of a moral argument. They who know that it does not hurt their faith to consume meat that has been sacrificed to idols, shall not use this knowledge in such a way that problems are created for those who do not (yet) understand this. Unfolded to a general principle, this means that our knowledge

3. Alfsvåg, *What No Mind Has Conceived*, 33–50.
4. McGrath, *Christian Theology: An Introduction*, 163–65.

is never definite and absolute, partly because it may have consequences we do not yet understand. It should therefore be used in such a way that it establishes and maintains fellowship both between God and humans and among humans. To achieve this goal, one must be humble on behalf of one's knowledge, and not be wise in one's own sight.

Augustine summarized this epistemology with another striking expression. He called it *docta ignorantia*, "informed ignorance."[5] We may be ignorant in different ways. We can be ignorant by being clueless, or we can be ignorant by not knowing as much as we think we know. Augustine is aiming at the kind of ignorance that has investigated all relevant sources and has thought the matter through in all its implications, and thus has arrived at the conclusion that one still has not grasped it. This is informed ignorance, and in his way, there is no other adequate epistemology.

This is a view of knowledge that invites a meditating attitude in relation to both nature and sacred texts. We find ourselves in a world we have not created; we are placed in a context we do not control. One may try to achieve control through full and unlimited knowledge of both situation and context, but this is not doable. Such a project can only induce conceit and arrogance. We will never proceed beyond the attempt at reflecting on what happens to us, and on the overarching contexts of which we may have an idea.

This is an epistemology with limitations. On this approach, the only thing one can know about God, is that God is not subject to the limitations that apply to everything else. As eternal and infinite, God is the unknowable Origin of the world we live in. Is God good? That is question that is not easily answered. The world is morally ambiguous. Here we find both love and abuse, both care and violence. What does this tell us about the world's Origin? Is it possible to believe in the ultimate victory of the good? Plato and his followers tried to answer that question by focusing on a basic difference between good and evil. We must know goodness to understand evil; evil appears as violation or absence of the good. This relation cannot be inverted; we cannot understand goodness as absence of evil. In the same way as darkness is absence of light and not the other way round, evil is goodness that has been disfigured. Therefore, Platonic philosophy thought it could defend the principle of the priority of the good. Is this philosophically defensible? And which help can be gained from philosophical reflections like these for persons who struggle with hardship and affliction?

---

5. Alfsvåg, *What No Mind Has Conceived*, 91

Another limitation of any meditating reflection on God's and the world's unknowability is that it is not a natural point of departure for finding precise theories and making accurate predictions. One may get a superficial and vague relation to the concrete problems of daily life, which is left to artisans and practicians who know how to do such things. From the fourteenth century, we have a philosophical school that found Augustine's *docta ignorantia*-principle unsatisfactory and tried to replace it with an approach that gave preference to precise, unambiguous knowledge. The most important representative of this school is the English philosopher and theologian William Ockham (1285–1347). The point of departure for this school of thought is that the world is composed of elements that can be precisely defined. This pertains both to God and everything else. This does not imply that the difference between God and the world disappears; God is still thought to have unique characteristics. However, God is no longer seen as the point of orientation that orders all knowledge. On the contrary, the demand for precise and unambiguous definitions is what structures the understanding of both God and the world. Human reason should in principle be able to grasp all of it. In this way, the human becomes the structuring center of the understanding of reality in way that is characteristically different from the Platonic-Augustinian tradition, where the human is seen as being at the receiving end of a reality it will never completely understand. The idea that the human may after all be able to get some understanding of the world is replaced by the idea that reality is what humans are able to think.[6]

The difference between the traditional and the new approach, which already by its contemporaries was called *via moderna* (the modern way) clearly surfaces in the understanding of creation. For the Platonic-Augustinian approach, creation is the point of departure of all knowledge. One can only grasp the adequate balance between what one knows and what one does not know by reflecting on the fact that what we try to understand is created by something beyond our comprehension. For the new and modern approach, the idea of creation is a possible inference that may or may not appear as the natural conclusion of the investigation of the world.[7] The idea of creation is no longer seen as the precondition for a consistent understanding of reality.

---

6. Broadie, *Duns Scotus and William Ockham*.
7. Kobusch, *Nominalismus*.

The moderns in this way tried to introduce a paradigm change that would allow for a more precise description of reality. It was, however, met with strong opposition from the old paradigm. The most important attempt at maintaining the Platonic-Augustinian approach was Luther's reformation. His theology of grace was an attempt at restoring the Platonic doctrine of unknowability as the philosophical point of orientation. According to Luther, our understanding of God cannot be built on our ability to establish an adequate understanding of God. It must be founded on God's one-sided and merciful giving of grace to humans. The Roman Catholic counter-reformation found its foundation in the thought of Thomas Aquinas (1225–74), who represents a compromise. He wanted to retain the tradition from Augustine, but in a form that was considered compatible with elements of the modern approach.

Even modern natural science had its background the Platonic-Augustinian understanding of reality. We can only have adequate knowledge of God to the extent that we have experienced God's reality. In the same way, we can only have adequate knowledge of the nature by experiencing it and describing and reflecting on what we have experienced. The call for an experience-based natural science therefore did not follow from the modern quest for precision, even if in due time it became important for interpreting and making use of the new knowledge of nature. Kepler's (1571–1630) laws for the movements of the planets, Galileo's (1564–1642) theory of motion and Newton's laws (1642–1726) were all examples of how the physical world could be precisely described by means of mathematical equations. Many thus concluded that only mathematical formulas satisfied the need for a precise description of reality, and this has been decisive for the understanding of reality for all modern humans. Ockham's suggestion for a paradigm change was ultimately victorious, even if it took four hundred years.[8]

The outcome was the modern preference for fact-based knowledge concerning the relations between phenomena that can be observed by humans and described mathematically. The experience of humans and the analysis of this experience became the engine in the production of knowledge. This vastly expanded our understanding in specific fields of knowledge, and through the modern technological revolution we have reaped the fruits of this development. At the same time, the field of knowledge was severely limited. The core of the Platonic-Augustinian, premodern understanding of

---

8. Henry, *Religion and the Scientific Revolution*; Hyman, *A Short History of Atheism*, 101–23.

reality, to see oneself and everything else illuminated by the relation to God who can never be captured in neat and unambiguous concepts, was no longer seen as relevant. This is a paradigm change with consequences far beyond the guilds of scholars. Not everybody will agree, though, that it represents an epistemological advance. The development may be more ambiguous than its adherents have been willing to admit.[9]

For theology and all faith-based understandings of reality, the paradigm change of modernity was a great challenge. They could no longer see the humans' relationship to their Creator as a given point of orientation for the understanding of reality. They therefore had to defend the significance of this approach by arguing from suppositions with a different foundation. Different churches and denominations did this in different ways, depending on how the challenge was understood. Within Protestantism, it led to a kind of theology that tried to defend its positions from the assumptions of the mathematically transparent, fact-oriented production of knowledge. Examples of this approach are nineteenth-century liberal theology, which defended faith in God by showing its ethical significance, and Rudolf Bultmann's (1884–1976) program of demythologization, which maintained that one has to eliminate the elements of traditional theology that are incompatible with the worldview of modernity.[10] In Bultmann's view, one should rather emphasize the proclamation of Jesus and the New Testament as helpful in the struggle to live an authentic life. Replacing the worldview that since Paul's speech at the Areopagus had been the context of Christian theology, had its challenges; important elements in its self-understanding had to be worked through in a new way.

The theology of modernity and its critics

The attempts at creating theology on the assumptions of modernity have provoked three kinds of reactions. The first one is the atheists' critique of the entire theological project. According to this critique, the quest for God can no longer be a meaningful enterprise. Traditional theology and the modern, science-based understanding of reality are incompatible entities. Even the Protestant attempts at reinventing theology should be rejected as

---

9. Three of the classics in the discussion of the significance of modernity are MacIntyre, *After Virtue*; Milbank, *Theology and Social Theory*; and Taylor, *A Secular Age*.

10. Bultmann, *New Testament and Mythology and Other Basic Writings*. The German original of the mythology-article was published in 1941.

just another way of putting "new wine into old wineskins"; the wineskins should preferably be thrown away.

The second approach is to take the modern methodological assumptions seriously, but still try to maintain the continuity with premodern theology to a greater extent than was done in nineteenth-century liberal theology and in the Bultmann school. I discussed one such approach in chapter 2, when I mentioned Pannenberg's openness toward Popper's falsification criterion, but without drawing a firm conclusion regarding the validity of Pannenberg's suggestion. We will have to conclude now.

The third approach is to reject the modern project by referring to its inherent ambiguities and contradictions. Is this the way to go to develop theology in dialogue with the contemporary worldview?

We will now have to discuss the objections against theology that are founded on the assumptions of modernity.

Atheism maintains that the word "God" is a word without reference; it refers to something that does not exist. As a replacement for the lacking reference, it gets its content from the desires and dreams of humans. Faith in God thus expresses nothing beyond the human desire for a better world, and for being recognized by a loving and caring divine Father. That faith in God is considered meaningful by its adherents can therefore not be an argument for the word "God" referring to reality. The study of religion is still interesting and important, because it teaches us a lot about human dreams and desires, but it will not tell us anything about God. This is a summary of the thought of the one of the first and most important atheists in European thought, Ludwig Feuerbach (1804–72).[11]

There were others who developed atheism in different directions. August Comte (1798–1857) maintained that religious models of explanation were something that were used in primitive societies lacking better models. Consequently, he thought that the growth of science would lead to the disappearance of religion. When one has understood the principles of modern meteorology, one will no longer explain thunder by referring to the hammer of Thor. Karl Marx (1818–83) agreed with Feuerbach and Comte that religion was a delusion, but he emphasized that it was a dangerous delusion. The mighty and powerful will invariably use religion to suppress the revolt of the powerless. By promising poor workers "a pie in the sky" (= a heavenly reward), one can prolong the structures of exploitation without doing anything to improve the situation. Sigmund Freud (1850–1929) thought

---

11. Feuerbach, *The Essence of Christianity*; German original published in 1841.

that faith in God is caused by psychological repression mechanisms. If these were resolved, faith in God would disappear. Both Comte, Marx, and Freud thought that faith in God would disappear when society became rationally transparent, even if they had quite different, and probably mutually exclusive, understandings of rationality.

Even Friedrich Nietzsche (1844–1900) maintained that faith in God was void of meaning. However, he was more interested in the implications of the lack of faith. In his view, there was a close connection between faith in God and the commandment to love one's neighbor.[12] Nietzsche evaluated this commandment in an extremely negative way and called it "the slave revolt in morality." He thought of this commandment as the revenge of the weak on the powerful. People who failed when trying to force their will on others had succeed in enforcing the rule that the powerful should show consideration for the weak. In Nietzsche's view, this was a common feature of Platonism and Christianity (which he called "Platonism for the people"). The disappearance of faith in God would lead to "a transvaluation of values." Love of one's neighbor and human equality will then not be relevant ideals anymore. The point is rather to make room for the strong and free individuals, who are their own divine authority.

The theories of Comte, Marx, and Freud can today be rejected as obsolete. Marx is right that religion may mask socially suppressive structures, but he is not right in maintaining that faith in God necessarily works in this way. There are many examples, both historical and contemporary, of faith in God serving as a motivation for work toward social justice. Comte and Freud were wrong when they thought that growth in knowledge would result in the disappearance of religion. As a theory of secularization, this is way too simple, and it has few adherents today.

Nietzsche's argument is much stronger. His insistence that with the abolishment of faith in God, everything will change, can hardly be challenged. However, this does not differ from what theology has always maintained; it is merely said from the other side. One's relationship to God is essential for the understanding of reality, and when the notion of God disappears as the point of orientation, everything changes. We cannot take it for granted that the idea of human equality—which is basic for all Western, liberal democracies—will remain once it is made independent of the faith in God that historically has been the presupposition of the idea. It is

---

12. Nietzsche, *On the Genealogy of Morality: A Polemic*; German original published in 1887.

unclear, however, whether Nietzsche's understanding of the significance of faith in God should be seen by us as an argument in favor of atheism or a critique of other atheists for not drawing the necessary conclusions from their atheism. If one does not believe in God, one cannot retain essential elements from the traditional, theologically grounded understanding of reality and morality without ending in contradictions. One can hardly disagree with Nietzsche in this respect.

In evaluating the validity of modernity's atheism, it is therefore still Feuerbach's argument that is the most interesting. Even this approach integrates elements from the Platonic-Augustinian tradition of negative theology. Plato, the Bible, Augustine, and Feuerbach agree when it comes to the critique of humanly created images of God. When atheism maintains that statements about God does not refer to reality, this concurs with traditional theology if "reality" is understood as referring to the created world within which we and our thoughts exist. Feuerbach's argument is thus reducible to the position that statements about God founded on the modern, anthropocentric, fact- and precision-based understanding of reality are invalid. Feuerbach maintains that this proves that all statements about God are invalid, but that is an unjustified conclusion. There is nothing in Feuerbach's argument that excludes the possibility that statements about God may be true if they refer to a reality outside and independent of the world to which we belong. It is therefore theologies based on Ockham's reorientation, which does not see God as the point of orientation that orders all knowledge, that is hit by Feuerbach's critique. The premodern, Platonic-Augustinian negative theology is beyond his horizon; it is not something he relates to.

This does not suggest that Plato is right, and Ockham is wrong. What it suggests is that they represent fundamentally different approaches to the world. There is therefore no neutral position from where these approaches may be evaluated. This is one of the implications of Kuhn's theory of paradigms, which I discussed in chapter 2. It suggests, however, that if Feuerbach's argument is valid, and I see no reason to disagree, it is hardly possible to develop a consistent theology from Ockham's presuppositions. To avoid contradictions, theology will have to understand itself as a reflection of the mystery of the world, maintaining the possibility that the world is to be understood as created by and anchored in an Origin we do not comprehend. Theology founded on this approach to reality will not understand atheist critique of religion as a rejection, but as a challenge to adhere to its own basic principles in a consistent way. Not only Nietzsche, but even Feuerbach is then more interesting as a dialogue partner than as a critic.

Atheism is right in the sense that humanly created images of God are inconsistent. But atheism is not right when it maintains that this nullifies all possibilities for a consistent and well-argued theology. This is possible if one is aware of the methodological restrictions that apply to theology as reflection on God's own reality. Since this possibility invariably is beyond what is considered by the defenders of atheism, it appears as an arbitrary loss of perspective. Nietzsche is an exception, because he tries to think the atheist project through and takes all its implications seriously. Few atheists follow him in this respect. For those who know the Platonic-Augustinian tradition of theology, atheism therefore often seems shallow and easily predictable. It does not produce new and surprising perspectives anymore.

However, even theology that takes the Platonic-Augustinian tradition as its point of departure will have to take Popper's falsificationism into account. In this respect, Pannenberg is undoubtedly right. Even theology works with analyses of historical facts and is therefore subject to the general criteria for academic accountability. But these criteria cannot be applied indiscriminately on theology intent on exploring the world's relationship to its unknowable Origin. The reason is that this kind of theology does not manifest itself in statements that specific elements in the world have certain properties; it is a project feeding on the fact that the world contains elements that have discernible properties and finds this to be most meaningfully interpreted as a witness of its divine Origin irrespective of the values of these properties. Theology understood in this way therefore cannot be empirically falsified; it should rather be seen as a suggestion of the preconditions for truth claims to be meaningful and falsifiable. It is thus a worldview that is confirmed by the fact that empirical falsifiability exists irrespective of its factual conclusions.

Theology as I am now exploring it thus questions whether the idea of meaning can be meaningfully maintained without the idea of God as an extra-worldly point of reference. As Plato claims in the *Republic*, we see what we see by the light of the sun. It therefore does not make sense to investigate phenomena in the world to see if the sun exists. Without the sun, phenomena in the world could not be investigated at all. According to the Neoplatonic and Christian interpretation of this parable, the notion of God and the doctrine of creation thus indicate the condition for formulating meaningful and justifiable statements about the world. As the exploration of precondition of the criterion of falsifiability, this project is in itself not falsifiable. Subjecting it to the criterion of falsifiability thus implies that one has left the Platonic-Augustinian paradigm and is working from Ockham's anthropocentric preconditions. This is certainly legitimate and may, under specific circumstances, even be commendable. However, it is not valid approach to a consistent way of doing theology. Understood as a theological paradigm, it is Ockham's project that appears as contradictory, because it replaces the meditative reflection on the works of God with human rationality as a rigorous frame for the understanding even of God. On Ockham's approach, it is only what appears as unambiguous according to the criteria of human rationality that can be recognized as real. Consistent theology cannot be maintained in this way.

Flew's critique of theology unwilling to accept the principle of falsifiability must therefore be rejected, but it is not irrelevant. The rejection can only be consistently upheld as long as theology maintains its self-understanding as reflection on divinity, and therefore considers divine unknowability an aspect of all it does. Theology is essentially not knowledge of facts, but a meditative reflection on the unknowability of God and the world. When this perspective is lost and theology is reduced to a collection of fact-based statements about God and the world, Flew's (and Feuerbach's) critique is again valid, and theology appears as wishful thinking.

Let me give a concrete example of the implication of this rather abstract discussion. A person may claim that he or she has experienced a divine intervention as answer to prayer. This is a statement that a certain event should be explained in a specific way and must therefore be testable to be trustworthy. How should it be tested? Should the experiment be repeated to see if the outcome is the same? The world is ambiguous, and what happens is not always good. If the expected result is missing when the experiment is repeated, how should this be interpreted? Is God then absent? Was the apparent answer to prayer just an arbitrary chain of events? If God is absent in this case, is he always absent, or rather non-existing, or did he refrain from doing the expected intervention just in this case? Is it at all possible to work with testable criteria for divine interventions? Flew's point is that questions like these invariably generate answers that are adjusted according to the occasion. He therefore concludes that they are arbitrary and uninteresting.

The actual event may, however, be described in a way that avoids Flew's criticism. This can be done by taking Plato, Paul, and Augustine seriously to the extent that one accepts that irrespective of what we experience and what we choose to present to God in prayer, we live and move in a God-given reality (cf. Acts 17:28). The aim of prayer is then not to give God the task of performing specific actions, the realization of which can be used to check God's existence and/or reliability. The aim of prayer is to help us to understand our experiences as the expression of divine presence irrespective of their outcome being humanly desirable or not. The relation to God describes a dimension of depth that is real without being testable through fact-based falsifications or verifications. It is undoubtedly the case that this is an attitude that can be of help when one is confronted by illness and other challenges. But one does not grasp the point by redefining theological statements to variations of the causal explanations of natural science, explanations that then have to be unendingly modified because the demand for falsification is never taken seriously.

In 1846, Søren Kierkegaard published a book he called *Concluding Unscientific Postscript*.[13] This is an extensive critique of the attempt at developing theology according to the principles of modern, fact-based science. In the first, fairly short part of the book, Kierkegaard's pseudonym, Johannes Climacus, rejects all attempts at doing this based on arguments for the historical reliability of the biblical account of revelation. Arguments for historical reliability will never prove anything beyond probability, and probability is not a relevant category for the encounter with God. It is not even a relevant category for a loving relationship between humans. In the encounter with God, one has to involve oneself without reservations or conditions. Climacus summarizes this in the claim that subjectivity is truth. This means that the question whether one relates to (eternal) truth or not, is determined by one's attitude. Truth requires a total commitment that does not take refuge in either arguments of probability or reflections on how others approach the problem of truth. The relation to God differs from all other relations, and we must all answer as individuals for our attitude towards this relation. It is only when one is aware of these realities that one's theology is adequate, according to Johannes Climacus.[14]

Kierkegaard was a contemporary of Feuerbach and knew his writings well. In *Philosophical Fragments*, which was published a few years before the *Postscript*, he lets Johannes Climacus evaluate Feuerbach's project.[15]

13. Kierkegaard, *Writings*, vol. 12/2.
14. Alfsvåg, *Christology as Critique*, 145–73.
15. Kierkegaard, *Writings*, vol. 12/1.

Climacus calls Feuerbach's critique of the Christian faith "an acoustic illusion." The reason is that Feuerbach's attack on the Christian faith actually amounts to a confirmation. By clearing away the kind of faith that is nothing but wishful thinking, he confirms the biblical critique of idolatry and opens a room for true faith. His critique is a kind of purification that lets the reality of a seasoned faith appear.[16]

Today, we are all modern in the sense that we have appropriated the modern worldview and collect its fruits through a control of the powers of nature that earlier generations only could dream of. We may then entertain the idea that the methods that give a precise, fact-based knowledge of the world should be helpful, even concerning the relationship to God. The fact that Christian theology through most of its history has thought differently must then be interpreted as the outcome of a way of thinking that now has become obsolete. However, the critique Kierkegaard and others have levelled against this belief in theological progress implies that methods developed for the sake of investigating and manipulating how phenomena in the world relate to each other will not be adequate for the exploration of the world's relation to its unknown origin.

---

16. Alfsvåg, *Christology as Critique*, 131.

4

What is the meaning of divine revelation?

Prophecy and incarnation

FEW HAVE REMAINED SATISFIED with the understanding of God expressed through the altar for the unknown God that Paul saw in Athens. Within all monotheistic faith traditions and many others, people have claimed to be able to say more without being inconsistent. That is only possible if God somehow has made himself known. Theology that wants to move beyond the understanding of God as the unknown Origin of all there is will therefore have to presuppose that God has revealed himself in ways that can be perceived and communicated in a methodologically consistent way. This again presupposes the existence of inspired receivers and communicators of divine revelation.

In the Bible, it is primarily the prophets who think of themselves as receivers and communicators of divine revelation, and they are quite conscious about this status (cf. Isa 50:4; Jer 1:9). They may not write after dictation, but they are clear that they proclaim a message of which they are not the origin (Amos 3:8). The inspired messages have been collected, written down, and transmitted as holy writings. The commandment to write may even be a part of the revelation (Jer 36:2–28). Therefore, all monotheistic faith traditions and many others have collections of holy writings that pass on divine revelation, and all have ideas of how the reception and the communication of the message may take place in ways that do not distort it.

Some will think this is impossible. They maintain that divine difference implies that God can never make himself known within the context of the created world. This is, however, a contradictory position. Taking divine difference seriously implies the impossibility of defining limits for what God can or cannot be thought to do. If God is Creator, he is also at home in the world, though still different from it. Divine self-revelation within the context of the created then certainly appears as a possibility.

However, the prohibition of idolatry and of self-made images of God establishes criteria for what can be considered divine revelation. It will never give an understanding of God's inmost essence. God's unknowability cannot be lifted without the distinction between God and creation being eliminated, as this would imply identity between human thoughts about God and the divine reality. However, revelation may give us an understanding of God's actions and how we may relate to them and to each other in a consistent way without the distinction between God and the world, or between God and humans, disappearing. This distinction even implies that, in relation to divine revelation, all humans are equal. Revelation can therefore not be used to elevate specific persons. This includes those who communicate the revelation (cf. Isa 6:5). If this principle is violated, the message that is communicated cannot trustworthily claim to be divine revelation. For the dialogue between religions these are important principles.

These are universally valid criteria. Christian faith still differs from other faith traditions by maintaining that God has not only inspired witnesses; *God has become a human being.* The promise of the incarnation was given to the prophets and is an important part of the Old Testament (Isa 9:6; Jer 23:6). The core of the New Testament message is the proclamation that this promise has been fulfilled. This can be expressed in a way that both connects with and transcends the understanding of divine unknowability that was discussed in chapter 3: "No one has ever seen God; the only God, who is at the Father's side, he has made him known" (John 1:18).

According to the Christian faith, the inspired prophets are therefore not the decisive communicators of revelation. The decisive revelation occurred, according to the Christian conviction, through *a specific person being the eternal God.* This solves a problem that always accompanies revelation through inspired prophets, since it is always difficult to know when the divinely inspired ends and is replaced by the merely human. When the revelation consists in God becoming human, the problem of distinguishing between the really divine and the merely human disappears: God is the revelation. At the same time, the project is both ambitious and paradoxical: how can one person be both eternal and infinite, and created and limited, at the same time?

WHAT IS THE MEANING OF DIVINE REVELATION?

Consequently, the incarnation is rejected by many, and this includes the most widely disseminated alternative version of monotheism, Islam. Within this faith tradition, divine incarnation is considered to be incompatible with the distinction between God and the world, a distinction both the Bible and the Quran maintain. The same position is held by some philosophical traditions, including Neoplatonism, which otherwise is quite close to Christianity. For this reason, it is the idea of incarnation that manifests the most important methodological challenge for Christian theology: how can one understand and communicate divine revelation primarily characterized by God becoming a human being while still maintaining divine difference, eternity, and unknowability in an adequate way?

Already the authors of the New Testament and, according to the Gospels, even Jesus himself are aware of the problem and have several strategies to solve it. It is unanimously maintained in the New Testament the Jesus should be understood as the revelation of the Old Testament prophecies of a future savior king (Matt 16:16-17; Mark 14:62; Acts 2:29-36). However, this is a description of the person of Jesus that is quite close to the description of the inspired prophet. Some therefore felt it necessary to add a description of the person of Jesus that unambiguously emphasizes his uniqueness as divine incarnation (Matt 11:27; John 10:30; 14:8-9). Exploring this aspect of the person of Jesus, the authors of the New Testament made use of the Jewish understanding of God's wisdom, through which the world was created according to the Old Testament (Prov 8:22-31). This was quite natural, as Jesus, according to the Gospels, intimated that he was the wisdom of God (Matt 11:19; 12:42). When translating the Jewish word for wisdom (*ḥākmâ*), they made use of the Greek word *lógos*, which means both "word" and "structure" (cf. our word "logic"). It is thus suitable for expressing both God's creation of the world through his word (cf. Ps 33:6; the Septuagint here has "The Lord's *lógos*"), and to describe Jesus as God's wisdom.

There are primarily three texts in the New Testament that use wisdom terminology to describe Jesus as God's incarnation: John 1:1-18; Col 1:15-20 and Phil 2:6-11. The introduction to the Gospel of John writes about God's *lógos*, which is eternal and divine, but was made flesh (*sárx*) and dwelt among us. It is obvious that the writer of the Gospel here is looking for terminology that lets him express what is characteristic for the person of Jesus, which he does by using words that strongly emphasize both its eternal and finite characteristics. The importance of emphasizing the physical and concretely fleshly is also underlined elsewhere in the Johannine writings (1 John 4:2; 2 John 7). The passage from Colossians presents Jesus as the image of God, but in a way that clearly is influenced by the Old Testament understanding of the wisdom of God as that through which the world was created. In the passage from Philippians, it is written in a similar way about Jesus who "was in the form of God" and was God's equal, but who humbled himself and became a servant and a human being. A fourth New Testament text, 1 Cor 8:6, connects the confession of faith in Jesus as Lord with the Old Testament confession of faith in the one God (Deut 6:4).

This gives a description of the person of Jesus that is complicated and not easily grasped by simple formulas. He is God and therefore eternal as God; he is the Son who is one with God the Father (John 10:30). At the same time, he is a concrete human being who lived among other humans. In the development of what we know as the Apostles' Creed (though it is not composed by the apostles), the church focused on Jesus as the fulfilment of the Messiah prophecies. The historical background of this creed is the baptizands' confession of faith, which according to the great commission in Matt 28:19 was a confession of faith in the Triune God: Father, Son, and Holy Spirit. It seems that the baptizands' confession of their faith in the Son was expanded by a summary of his life to show him as the fulfilment of the prophecies: he was born by a virgin, suffered under Pontius Pilate, died, was buried and rose again. Isaiah 53 has probably been important when the creed was structured like this, because these are the exact elements (birth, suffering, death, burial, and resurrection) that are emphasized in this text. In addition, the Apostles' Creed contains one expression that points beyond the merely messianic, and that is the understanding of Jesus as the only-begotten Son, which is a quotation from John 1:18.

The development ending in the Apostles' Creed took place in the Latin-speaking part of the early church and was quite uncontroversial. Within the Greek-speaking church it was considerably more difficult to maintain the fullness of the New Testament description of Jesus in a way that was accepted by all. This led to extensive debates on what is called Christology (the doctrine of the person of Jesus). The word is derived from *Christós*, which is the Greek translation of *Messiah*, meaning "The Anointed One" (= the king).

Among some Jewish Christians, Jesus was understood as the fulfilment of the messianic prophecies in a way that led them to consider him an inspired prophet. When Jesus was baptized, he received the Spirit of God in a way that enabled him to complete his work as the Savior of humans. The problem with this approach, which is called adoptionist Christology (because it understands Jesus as God's adopted Son) is that it cannot integrate the understanding of Jesus as the pre-existent, eternal Son of God who existed already before he was conceived in his mother's womb. This understanding of Jesus's divinity is something that is particularly emphasized in the Gospel of John.

Other Christians were inspired by Greek and Hellenistic ideas of the physical as sinful and understood material creation as a fall to a lower, more material way of life from which it was important to be liberated. This is a common characteristic for groups usually gathered by scholars under the label Gnosticism. Taking this as one's point of departure, it is difficult to make sense of Jesus as *truly* human, because that would demean him. This approach leads to what is called docetic Christology (from Greek *dokeîn*, "to appear"), because according to this interpretation, Jesus merely *appeared* to be human. However, this cannot be aligned with the understanding of Jesus as *sárx* (flesh), which is so strongly emphasized in the Johannine writings.

Neither adoptionism nor docetism could therefore remain as unifying conclusions. They were not sufficiently sophisticated to maintain the complexity of the descriptions of Jesus in the New Testament. They were too strongly influence by a human way of thinking to capture the paradox of the eternal God appearing as a human being.

The discussion that ultimately clarified the significance of the understanding of the person of Jesus for theology's self-understanding was the discussion that originated with the position of Arius from Alexandria (250–336). His starting point was a strict understanding of God's eternity and indivisibility similar to what was found in Neoplatonism (and later in Islam). In his view, it is inconsistent to suppose the existence of two, not to say three, eternal, divine persons. If God is eternal and infinite, God is also indivisible. Then Jesus cannot be eternal in the same sense as God is eternal. Arius accepted the understanding of Jesus as pre-existent, but as he saw it, God first created the Son, who subsequently was involved in the creation of everything else. Arius thought he could find exegetical arguments supporting this view. Does not Proverbs 8:22 say that the creation of wisdom was the first of God's acts? Does not Colossians 1:15 tell us that the Son is "the firstborn of all creation"?

The most important opponent of Arius was Athanasius (296–373), and he had three objections against the Christology of Arius. Firstly, God's wisdom must be as eternal as God, for God cannot be thought to exist without his wisdom. Proverbs 8:22 must therefore be understood as a figural way of expressing the divine wisdom's eternal origin in God. Secondly, it is only God who can save us. If Jesus undialectically is understood as a part of the created world, he cannot be a Savior. Thirdly, the church has always worshipped Jesus as God. The Gospels tell us about the first times the prayer *kýrie eléēsón* (Lord, have mercy!) was addressed to Jesus (Matt 15:22; 17:15; 20:30-31), and this has always been a part of the church's liturgy. Meeting Jesus after the resurrection, Thomas calls him "My Lord and my God" (John 20:28). If Jesus is not God, but merely a part of the created world, this would be idolatry and a violation of the first commandment. However, neither Jesus nor the apostles understood it this way. Colossians 1:15 can therefore not be interpreted in the way Arius interprets it.[1]

The debate concerning the Christology of Arius was lengthy and disruptive. It lasted for generations, and two councils were summoned to solve the problem (in Nicaea in 325 and in Constantinople in 381). Eunomius (d. 393), one of the leading Arians in the time after Arius, held that God cannot generate any other besides himself. By the term "ungeneracy" one gets to know God essentially. His opponent Gregory of Nyssa (about 335–95) objected that it was incompatible with the principle of divine unknowability to maintain that there are concepts defining God essentially. In the beginning of this chapter, I maintained that a rejection of the possibility of divine revelation is incompatible with the principle of divine difference; it is impossible for humans to define what God can or cannot do. In his critique of Eunomius, Gregory applied the same principle. One cannot limit the field of possible divine acts to exclude the possibility of incarnation. Divine difference must be understood to include even the possibility of God becoming one of us without his difference being affected by it. If God is infinite and unknowable, it must be possible for him to be both one of us and infinitely different at the same time. If not, our understanding of divine difference is not sufficiently radical.[2]

Logically, this is impossible. However, both infinity and incarnation expand the area of the possible as far as God is concerned. The possibility that it cannot be captured or limited by human logic must therefore be seen

---

1. Hägglund, *History of Theology*, 80–85
2. Alfsvåg, *What No Mind Has Conceived*, 40–43.

WHAT IS THE MEANING OF DIVINE REVELATION?

as real. Infinity implies indefinability; God can in the core of his essence never be captured by human thought structures. As far as the understanding of God is concerned, reason can therefore never be the final judge. This is an essential point in the critique Athanasius and Gregory of Nyssa directed against Arius and Eunomius.

The creed that was the outcome of the two councils that discussed the Arian controversy is called the Nicene Creed (though in the form we now use it, it was not composed at Nicaea). The central text around which the Apostles' Creed developed is Matt 28:19. The core text around which the Nicene Creed developed is Paul's Christocentric application of Deut 6:4 in 1 Cor 8:6: We believe in one God..., we believe in one Lord.... This Creed summarizes the life of Jesus in a way that closely resembles the Apostles' Creed, but adds a more precise description of the relation between the Father and the Son by means of images and metaphors from the wisdom Christology of the New Testament. The Son is "begotten from the Father before all ages" (he is not created in time, and therefore not a part of the created world), "God of God" (cf. John 1:1), "light from light" (a combination of John 8:12 and 1 John 1:5), "true God from true God" (cf. Col 1:15a; Phil 2:6), "begotten, not made" (cf. Heb 1:5).[3]

However, the Nicene Creed includes one philosophical concept that is not taken from the New Testament: The Son is "of one being (Greek *homooúsios*) with the Father." The Arians were skeptical and wanted to use only biblical expressions. The council fathers still felt they had to use it to stop the Arians from interpreting all biblical texts and expression in accordance with their own principles, the indivisibility of God and the understanding of Jesus as created. The *homooúsios*-concept was thus accepted as a part of the Nicene Creed to guard the biblical metaphors against what the council fathers considered a misinterpretation. The Father and the Son are one (cf. John 10:30) even if the Son is incarnated and the Father is not. We cannot grasp this rationally and logically, but this is how the biblical authors tell the story, and this is how the church has confessed her faith since the time of the apostles. Therefore, this is a part of the distinctive character of the Christian church and of Christian theology. It is anchored in the biblical stories and in the interpretations the texts of the Bible give of these stories. This reflects God's own reality and should therefore not be limited by presuppositions for knowability and consistency collected from the created world.

3. Kolb and Wengert, *The Book of Concord*, 22–23.

The main objection against this approach is that dispensing with logical consistency as a criterion for truth will lead to arbitrariness. If faith is not related to something that holds together logically, cannot then anything be considered genuine faith? This worry is probably behind Arius' and Eunomius' attempts at arriving at a kind of Christology that allows for a less ambiguous and more precise and conceptually univocal understanding of God. Athanasius and Gregory reject the objection, and the Nicene Creed is created from the presupposition that this rejection is crucial. However, the rejection of the possibility of capturing God by logic does not imply that anything can be said. The prohibition of idolatry still stands. Statements about God that confuse divine and created reality are always unacceptable. At the same time, incarnation opens the possibility of speaking about God's presence in the world in a new way. In Jesus, God identifies with parts of the created world. What is created is qualified as an area for divine presence in a way that would not have been possible without the incarnation. What is said about God's presence in the world, will thus have to be qualified by the story of Jesus. If not, one opens the door to arbitrariness in the understanding of God.

The conclusion of the fathers of the early church was that it is possible to develop a methodologically consistent Christian way of thinking from these presuppositions. The essential requirement is that God's incarnation in Christ is considered the point of orientation for the understanding of reality.

The significance of Christology for the understanding of reality

The Nicene Creed is the most ecumenically recognized and widely used Creed in the Christian church. The conclusion of the church fathers in the Arian controversy has thus shown itself to be exceptionally strong and stable. However, the methodological implications of this conclusion have never been obvious and uncontested. Through the history of the church, the implications of faith in Jesus as truly God and truly human for theology's understanding of itself have repeatedly been discussed.

This was the case already for the first generations after the Council of Constantinople. The Arians were now marginalized. All who took part in this debate accepted that, according to the New Testament, Jesus must be understood both as *fully God* and *fully human*. The discussion was concerned with the implication of this view for the understanding of the person of Jesus. How can one person be both God and man, and how are we to describe this person more precisely?

There were two main parties in this discussion. The main representatives of one of them came, like both Arius and Athanasius, from Alexandria. The Alexandrians understood the divinity of Jesus to be the integrating principle of his person. Jesus is God who has become human; he is not a human who has become God. The more one-sided expressions of this view are called monophysitism (from Greek *phýsis* = nature) or one nature-doctrine. Jesus is a divine-human. The critics maintained that this did not allow for a sufficiently real understanding of the human nature of Jesus. Would his experiences of hunger, illness, and anxiety then be real? Does he have an independent human will? If that is not the case, is Jesus then a fellow human being "who in every respect has been tempted as we are" (Heb 4:15)?

The other party had its geographical center in Antioch in Syria and had a more Bible-based approach. They looked at the stories of Jesus in the Gospels and noticed that one here could find both divine and human attributes. Jesus was hungry and thirsty, he wept at the tomb of Lazarus (John 11:35), and he fought with fear of death in the garden of Gethsemane. This shows that Jesus was a human being, and we recognize ourselves in his experiences. At the same time, he proclaimed the will of God with authority, he performed miracles and conquered death. This shows us the divine attribute of the person of Jesus. In the Gospels, we thus clearly see *both* the divine *and* the human aspects of the person of Jesus, and this was well expressed by the Antiochians. However, according to its critics, this party had no adequate way of expression the unity of the person of Jesus. The Antiochians thus worked with a two-persons' model of Jesus, one divine and one human, to the extent that the mysterious unity of the two tended to disappear.

Eventually, the discussion narrowed down to the question whether the virgin Mary should be called the Mother of God (in Greek *theotókos*). To be born by a woman is typically human attribute; this can be said about all of us. The Alexandrians held that since, according to the Gospels, it was the Son of God who was conceived in Mary (cf. Luke 1:32 and 35) and thus also born by her, she could truly be called Mother of God. Nestorius (386–450), who came from Antioch and was elected patriarch in Constantinople in 428, suggested, as a compromise, that one could say that Mary bore Christ. This was not a good idea, as he then became the target of criticism from both sides.

Because he in this way became the center of the battle, one has often used his name for the Antiochians and called them Nestorians.[4]

As with the Arian controversy, two councils were needed to solve the disagreement between monophysites and Nestorians. The important one was the last of them, which took place in Chalcedon (like Nicaea situated in the vicinity of Constantinople) in 451. The decision of this council confirmed the significance of the Nicene Creed by explicitly accepting the Christology of the councils of the preceding century. The Council of Chalcedon then confirmed both the divinity and humanity of Jesus without limitations, making it more precise by adding that Jesus has both a humanly rational soul and a body, and by applying the *homooúsios*-concept even on the human nature of Jesus. He is thus also "of one being" with us. Jesus is not a divine person with some human attributes; he is fully human and fully divine at the same time.

This was, however, merely a repetition of the position of the Nestorians. What is really interesting is to see how the council then solved the problem of unity of the person. The solution is simply to declare the problem to be unsolvable. About Jesus we can only say that he is *one person* with *two natures*. This is the only way to capture the complexity of the New Testament expressions, and we will never be able to proceed beyond this point. This solution was recommended by Tertullian (about 150–240) more than two hundred years before the Council of Chalcedon, but since he wrote in Latin, his suggestion did not influence the discussion among the Greeks before being introduced in that context before the council. This is in principle the same solution as the one we have in the Nicene Creed concerning the relation between the Father and the Son. We can only repeat the biblical expressions; there is no other way of doing this.

To strengthen this conclusion, the decision of the council takes one more step and explicitly rejects two possible interpretations of the relationship between Jesus's two natures. This is, the council's text says, a relation *without confusion* and *without separation*. The text uses four negative adverbs to describe how not to think about the relation between the natures: Jesus is "acknowledged in two natures, inconfusedly, unchangeably, indivisibly, inseparably" (the Latin translation says *inconfuse, immutabiliter, indivise, inseparabiliter*).[5]

---

4. Hägglund, *History of Theology*, 90–100.
5. Schaff, *The Creeds of Christendom*, vol. 2, 62–63.

The union thus does not take away the differences of the natures. Jesus is not a divine-human in the sense that he is a little of both, e.g., by understanding his divinity as a metaphor for his power and knowledge. The word may be used in this way; we may say about a work of art or an extraordinary experience that they are "absolutely divine." The Chalcedon-decision goes the extra mile to emphasize that this is *not* how the divinity of Jesus should be understood. He is the eternal God, fully and without modification. In the same way, he is also fully human. Here the council follows the Nestorians over against the monophysites.

The incarnation implies that the divine and the human are united in the person of Jesus in such a way that this union is inseparable. Jesus is *always* fully divine and human. On this point, the council follows monophysitism over against Nestorianism. Consequently, the council says that it is correct to say that Mary is the Mother of *God*, because the child conceived in her and born by her was the eternal God. This implies that the stories of the ascension of Jesus (Mark 16:19; Luke 24:51; Acts 1:9) should not be taken to imply that Jesus puts off his humanity and returns to God's heaven. The ascension is the enthronement of the God-man Jesus, which implies that our brother, the man Jesus, now returns to his position at the right hand of the Father to pray for us, his brothers and sisters (Heb 2:17; 7:25).

In the discussion that followed the Council of Chalcedon, the inseparable union of human and divine in Christ was maintained through reflections of what is summarized in the Latin expression *communicatio idiomatum*, which means communication of properties. Because the created and uncreated are inseparably united in Jesus, the created and the uncreated through the incarnation participate in each other's properties. This is helpful when we are confronted by problems that may be intellectually challenging. One of them is the understanding of the death of Jesus at the cross. If Jesus is true God, does the death of Jesus imply that God died? This is called patripassianism (God the Father suffered and died at the cross). How does this then relate to the biblical idea of divine unchangeability (Jas 1:17)? Can the world persist if its Creator and Preserver dies? The doctrine of *communicatio idiomatum* implies that through the incarnation, the divine nature participates in the human property mortality, and may thus suffer death without its unchangeability being affected. The differences of the divine nature do not disappear. This does not give us a complete understanding of the event, but it gives us a possibility of articulating the problem without having to choose between two unacceptable alternatives. The death of Jesus at the cross neither implies that he only dies according to his human nature, nor does it imply that the unchangeable God dies.

In the same way, the human nature of Jesus participates in the divine property omnipresence or ubiquity. Consequently, Jesus can promise his presence without restrictions and conditions (Matt 18:20; 28:20). The one who is ubiquitously present after the resurrection is thus the *same* as the one who was with his disciples during his ministry. This is suggested already by the resurrection stories telling us the resurrected Jesus has a physical body (Luke 24:39–43; John 20:27) that can pass through closed doors (John 20:19). The presence of Jesus on earth after resurrection and ascension is therefore not a merely spiritual presence. It is a bodily presence, though without some the limitations that pertain to our bodies. This even allows for an understanding of the omnipresence of the Creator without the difference between Creator and creation being abolished.

Both the Nicene Creed's understanding of the relation between the Father and the Son and the two-nature Christology of the Council of Chalcedon were conceived within the appreciation of divine unknowability that was unfolded in chapter 3. The natures are united without their properties disappearing. Two-nature Christology does not abandon divine unknowability but maintains it in a more precise way. God, who creates the light that illuminates everything, lives in an unapproachable light (1 Tim 6:16). He has, however, appeared before us as a human being without cancelling or weakening his divinity. The eternal and infinite one becomes a human being and is still the eternal and infinite (John 1:18). The tools that stand to our disposal through our experiences and our mastery of language can only refer to these mysteries through allusions and figural expressions. We "see in a glass, darkly." If we try to escape this limitation by striving for univocity and unambiguity in the way we speak about God's incarnation, our only achievement will be the disappearance of the phenomenon we are struggling to explain.

An important implication of the union of God and humanity in the person of Jesus without their differences disappearing is that God and the created, or God and the human, cannot be understood as opposites. God and the created cannot be described through a fixed set of questions with different answers, as the understanding of the one, in practice the infinite, will then be structured on the presuppositions of the other, in practice the created. The incarnation means that divine difference does not imply that God and the created are negative images of each other, so that the one is what the other is not. This was Arius' position; his conclusion was that a part of the created (a human being) cannot be God in an unlimited way without the nature of God being altered. According to Arius, God and human are opposites who cannot participate in each other's existence without their respective properties being abandoned. Gregory of Nyssa and the council fathers in the fourth century came to the opposite conclusion. If God is infinitely different from the created, he can include the created in himself without his infinity and unchangeability being affected. When we are dealing with infinity, the rules are different. If we consider this unacceptable, we are not dealing with infinity, but something that resembles it in some respects. The New Testament revelation tells us that God in his infinity has made use of the finite and created to tell us who he is. There are no logically compelling reasons for accepting this, as infinity and logically compelling reasons are incompatible entities. Faith can therefore never be enforced by rationally compelling arguments. On the other hand, the possibility of the incarnation can hardly be rejected without contradiction, as a rejection of the possibility of the incarnation implies a limitation of the infinite according to the limiting suppositions of human rationality.

The incarnation thus implies that the created is employed as the area for divine presence. This seems to be a natural thing to do; after all, the incarnated one is the Origin of the world. However, modernity's demand for univocity and unambiguity has questioned this approach and renewed a way of thinking that is closely related to Arius's. If one adheres to a principle of univocity and definability in relation to both God and the world to the extent that everything should be describable through unambiguous concepts, then both God and the world will have to be defined, and for that reason limited, in relation to each other. Then God's presence in the world can no longer be seen as a material, embodied presence, and the concretely material cannot be understood to participate in God in an unknowable and ineffable way. Taking this as one's point of departure, one can only think of God as present in a non-material way, i.e., as spirit.

Both in the early church and in the Middle Ages we see the beginnings of a conflict between an incarnation-based and a more spiritual way of conceiving of God's presence in the world. At the time of the Reformation, though, the conflict became acute. It was the sixteenth century's most consistent anti-modernist Martin Luther who both had the most radical understanding of the infinite and at the same time insisted on the materiality of divine presence in the shape of oral and written words and the bread and wine of the Lord's Supper.[6] The Roman Catholics were skeptical to the former concretization; Zwinglians and Calvinists to the latter. The Romans held that the church's leadership had a spiritual knowledge beyond what could be read in the holy books; they therefore maintained that they alone could provide the correct interpretation of the Bible. The Zwinglians (who got their name from Ulrich Zwingli, 1484–1531) held that the words of Jesus when he instituted the Lord's Supper ("this is my body; this is my blood") should be understood as a figure of speech directing our attention to Jesus giving his life for us on the cross. There was thus no material presence of divinity. Jean Calvin agreed with Luther and the Roman Catholics that this was a dubious interpretation of the text. He was still skeptical towards Luther's radical exposition of the idea of *communicatio idiomatum*, though. Applied on the understanding of the Lord's Supper, it implies that Jesus is physically present in the shape of bread and wine. In Calvin's view, a human cannot be omnipresent. He therefore thought that Jesus can only be present in the Lord's Supper in a spiritual way. But, according to Luther and his supporters, this distinction amount to a kind of Nestorianism. The question is: does the Calvinist differentiation of the modes of presence of Jesus's natures incorporate the emphasis of the Council of Chalcedon of the inseparability of the divine and the human in the person of Jesus?

However, the challenges for an incarnation-based understanding of reality, which sees the world as the area for divine presence based on the union of divine and human in Jesus, became even stronger after the Enlightenment. Basic for post-Enlightenment modernity is the understanding of reality as unambiguously reducible to a mathematically describable univocity. Modernity's understanding of the spiritually dead nature has therefore fittingly been described as "disenchantment."[7] One can then only relate to divinity in the same way as one relates to the mathematically describable, physical reality, e.g., by accepting the criterion of falsifiability as relevant even for theology (cf. the discussion of this problem in chapter 3). The alternative is to understand God as pure spirituality. God and the world then become opposites as in Arius and Zwingli. Protestant theology under modernity by and large has followed the latter alternative.

Immanuel Kant (1724–1804), who is the philosopher of modernity par excellence, found a room for God by understanding him as the origin of morality. The idea of divine unknowability thus disappears. On Kant's

---

6. Alfsvåg, *Christology as Critique*, 48–52.
7. Taylor, *A Secular Age*, 25–26.

WHAT IS THE MEANING OF DIVINE REVELATION?

presuppositions, the idea of God is quite rational; God is the warrant for the belief that eventually the good ones are rewarded, and the evil ones are punished. Admittedly, there remains an unknowability problem even in Kant, but the understanding differs from what we find in the Platonic-Augustinian tradition. In Kant, unknowability appears in form of the distinction between the world *in itself* ("Ding an sich"; unknowable) and the world *as it appears for us* ("Ding für mich"; knowable). For Kant, the structuring center of the understanding of reality is thus the knowing subject, not, as in premodern Platonism, the world and its unknown origin.[8] Kant described this as a Copernican revolution in the world of thought; he thus considered it to be as radical as the transition from a geocentric to a heliocentric worldview. Still, he arguably just drew the logical conclusion of the paradigm change suggested by Ockham.

Kant's younger colleague G. W. F. Hegel (1770–1831) solved the problem of the relation between God and the world in another way. He was interested in historical development, which in his view primarily occurs in the area of the intellectual or spiritual. His disciple Marx later changed this, considering material development essential, but Hegel never contemplated this possibility. For Hegel, the task of the human is to capture the spirit of history by getting a sense of the essence of and the relationship between the different epochs. In this way, one could capture how God as the absolute spirit manifests himself through history. There is thus no clear difference between the eternal and the created in Hegel's thought. For Hegel, the divine or the spiritual is just another way of expressing what we with a Hegel-inspired phrase call the "spirit of the time." This spirit is in principle knowable, at least if one takes the time required to read Hegel's voluminous writings and then interpret history accordingly.

Both Kant and Hegel in this way keep the door open for theology and spirituality without rejection the basic principles of modernity. They were therefore attractive as dialogue partners for the theologians, and later Protestant theology is clearly influenced by this discussion with Kant and Hegel. This led to a spiritualization of the God-relationship that created a turning point within the history of Christian thought. Christian thinkers from the church fathers to the Reformers found attempts at exploring the significance of Christology for the understanding of reality to be of utmost importance. This presupposes that the difference between Creator and creation is maintained as the absolute point of orientation while the possibility

---

8. Tyson, *Returning to Reality*, 160–61.

of a material manifestation of the divine within the area of created is retained. An understanding of the God-relationship as purely spiritual, based on either Kant, Hegel, or New Age-inspired attempts at applying the religious traditions of the East as alternatives to Western one-sidedness, are founded on a different worldview.

For theology under modernity, two-nature Christology and its insistence on *communicatio idiomatum* as the key to the understanding of reality, thus becomes a stumbling block. The physical world is not God's place anymore. God is either found in a particular area of spirituality or morality, or he is simply neglected. The merit of modern Protestantism is that it has succeeded in maintaining theology as a meaningful academic enterprise under these circumstances. The critical question to be asked is whether this is an adequate form of Christian theology. Can and should Christian theology do without two-nature Christology as the key to the understanding of the world?

Pannenberg deserves credit for having tried to overcome this tendency toward spiritualization, but as I have argued in chapter 3, his attempt must be considered inconsistent. We have a much more radical critic of the modern project in Søren Kierkegaard. He is adamant that if the continuity of Christian theology is to be preserved, we must reject both modernity's demand for unambiguity and the implicated spiritualization of the God-relationship. He also rejects Hegel's attempt at developing a philosophical theology by reading off the development of the spirit of history. If humans for the sake of mastering the universe must abandon what Kierkegaard calls "the infinite qualitative difference" between God and human, then humans make themselves the center of the understanding of reality in a way that is highly problematic, both philosophically and theologically. In Kierkegaard's view, this represents a kind of hubris he can only treat with exquisite irony.

As Kierkegaard sees it, it is more adequate to accept the radicality of the incarnation with all its implications. In the two writings I have already referred to, Kierkegaard's pseudonym Johannes Climacus explores how the incarnation, which he calls "the God in time," presents us with the ultimate challenge, and how one can only relate adequately to this challenge by not yielding to the demand for a complete understanding of reality. The decisive battles are always fought on an arena where we never have the full perspective.

WHAT IS THE MEANING OF DIVINE REVELATION?

Kierkegaard's contemporaries were largely deaf to his message, at least as far as the theologians are concerned. They found it impossible to ground the understanding of reality in two-nature Christology as Luther and Kierkegaard had done. There was, however, a new interest in Kierkegaard in the twentieth century, partly due to the fact that Karl Barth (1886–1968) renewed some of Kierkegaard's emphases, though Barth himself was influenced by the understanding of God and human as opposites to the extent that he never quite grasped the incarnation-based paradoxes in the thought of Luther and Kierkegaard. Still, he has been important for a renewal of the insight that theology that takes itself seriously and hopes to be taken seriously by others must insist that it explores divine revelation and speaks on God's behalf. Whether this is met with opposition or acclamation is eventually uninteresting. Theology wanting to proclaim divine revelation will never receive its mandate from the spirit of the time. On this point, Kierkegaard and Barth agreed completely.

5

How does one become a theologian?

Reasoning, self-understanding, and spirituality

THIS BOOK HAS SO far discussed the content of theology. Taking an understanding of God informed by the doctrines of creation and incarnation as my point of departure, I have explored the identity of theology, its content, the presuppositions and implications of this content, and how it should relate to the contemporary context. However, we will also have to look at those who study theology and appropriate its content. How is a theologian formed and educated?

I chapter 1, I defined theology as scholarly work concerning the God-relationship that takes the understanding of the reality of the faith tradition seriously. It therefore makes sense that the education of theologians since the establishment of the European universities in the Middle Ages has taken place in an academic context. An important part of theology is the understanding of what it is to be human. Theology will therefore have implications for the self-understanding of those who study it. This gives theology an existential dimension most university subjects lack, even if theology is not alone in having this dimension. In addition, the relationship to God has a practice dimension we call spirituality. Believers relate to God through prayer and worship, both individually and collectively. The education of theologians therefore has cognitive, existential, and liturgical-spiritual dimensions.

We find these dimensions already in the Bible. Jesus emphasizes the existential dimension of the God-relationship: "If anyone would come after me, let him deny himself and take up his cross and follow me" (Matt 16:24); "if anyone's will is to do God's will, he will know whether the teaching is from God or whether I am speaking on my own authority" (John 7:17). The message of Jesus can only be accepted through personal involvement. The connection between understanding and spirituality is emphasized in Ps 111:10: "The fear of the LORD is the beginning of wisdom." The significance of prayer and worship is one of the governing ideas of the Bible. Rules for worship is an important part of the Pentateuch, the Book of Psalms is the prayer book of the Old Testament congregation, and the glimpses we get of the heavenly glory show us the worship before the throne of God (Isa 6:2–3; Rev 7:9–11).

This unity of the intellectual, the spiritual, and the personal appropriation was, in the first centuries of the history of Christian church, maintained by the education of what we would now call theologians taking place in the congregations. The basic level was the preparation for baptism, and this was followed by a kind of higher education where participation in the life of the congregation was the essential part. Normally, there was no sharp distinction between the education of believers and the education of the church's leadership. Obviously, there were people who distinguished themselves by having a better grasp of theological problems than believers in general. Some of these had graduated from the ordinary institutions of higher learning and brought that education into the church and developed it. Both Augustine and other church fathers were educated in rhetoric. This system had its weaknesses; there was no system in place to ensure the formal competence of the leadership of the church. The recruitment of priests and bishops therefore happened in ways we today would consider somewhat haphazard. Still, there is no doubt the church had leaders who were highly educated and used their education in the church in a very constructive way. The level of precision and insight among the best of the church fathers was astonishingly high.

The organization of the production of theological knowledge changed somewhat with the establishment of the medieval monasteries. The essential part of monastic life was time in prayer, both collectively and individually, the Book of Psalms being the central prayer book. The production of theological knowledge in the monasteries was therefore mainly meditative Bible expositions coming from a praying fellowship. Monasticism established a distinction between common Christians and distinctly spiritual Christians, though there is no doubt that many monasteries were spiritual centers that raised the level of theological knowledge and spirituality in the church.

There were no significant controversies concerning the inner aspect of the faith life in the early church. This does not imply that the subject was found uninteresting. On the contrary, the education of believers with an emphasis on the call to follow the Lord through a life in prayer and participation in the life of the congregation was strongly emphasized. The great debates were on the understanding of creation and incarnation. Indirectly, this discussion influenced spirituality and faith life, as the fellowship of the believers with Christ through the sacramental life of the church was considered essential. It would therefore have been natural for Athanasius to use the believers' worship of Christ as an argument in the Arian controversy. The understanding of the relationship between God and the believer still does not surface as a separate element of the discussion.

The first time it does in a way that makes a lasting impression is in the debate between Augustine and Pelagius (360–418) on the content and preconditions of a life in faith. Augustine wanted to give the life in faith a platform that could nourish and strengthen both faith and obedience and was one of the advocates of what became the monastic movement. In his great spiritual autobiography *Confessiones* he shows a level of psychological self-investigation that is unparalleled among authors of antiquity. He is well aware of his own weaknesses and propensity for yielding to temptations. He therefore knew from his own experience his dependence on a living relationship with God for the soundness of his faith life. He summarizes this in the following prayer, quoted in *Confessiones*: "Give what you command and command what you will," to which he adds the comment that his only hope is in God's "exceeding great mercy."[1] Obedience and the forming of himself as a believer and theologian presuppose an imploring spirituality, where faith continually seeks renewal in the silence before God and thus receives what God gives as the foundation of the life in faith.

Pelagius considered this an invitation to spiritual laziness. He was fed up with believers who used the grace of God as a pretext for rejecting the reality of the command to follow Jesus. In Pelagius's view, the believers should struggle to follow God's commands and not hide their dislike for them behind pious expressions, which he often found to be the case. We have received the commandments to follow them, and we have no reason to believe that this is impossible. When God tells us to renounce wealth and sensual pleasure and not be disturbed by what obscures his will for us, he wants us to take this seriously. What is important is to make a decision to let one's life be governed by God's commandments and live accordingly.

---

1. *Confessiones* XXIX.40, quoted from Augustine, *Confessions*.

Pelagius and his followers did not reject the doctrine of salvation through baptism. However, they did not accept an understanding of sin as an invincible power. They therefore considered the grace of God to be revealed primarily through the revelation of his will. Now our task is to follow the instructions. There may be a new possibility for those who have erred, though Pelagius has no patience for those who repeatedly return to God with their transgressions. In his view, these people have not taken their conversion seriously.

Augustine, too, thought that the commands should be taken seriously, and Pelagius and his followers could therefore defend themselves against critique by pointing to Augustine's writings. Augustine therefore had to involve himself in the discussion. His view was that Pelagius, despite his Augustine-quotations, was seriously wrong. The human proclivity for rejecting the divine command of love as the rule of conduct is not something one can just decide to put away. On the contrary, the Bible tells us that we are captured by an inclination to evil from which we cannot liberate ourselves (cf. Paul's list of Old Testament quotations in Rom 3:10-12). To be saved is to be liberated from this inclination to the effect that one will live a life in obedience. This liberation can only be accomplished through an act of God. Consequently, the Bible does not understand divine grace as a piece of information one can decide to consider important or to overlook. Divine grace is an act of God, which in the Bible is described as a new creation (2 Cor 5:17; Gal 6:15). One receives a new mindset. Jesus therefore emphasizes that the relation to himself he wants his disciples to have must be given by God (John 6:44). To clarify the significance of the divine action, both the Old and the New Testaments repeatedly describes the creation of a trusting relationship to God as the result of an election, the subject of which is always God (Deut 7:6; 14:2; Isa 41:8; Matt 24:22, 24, 31; Acts 13:48; Rom 8:28-30; 11:5; 1 Pet 1:2). This election is a decision from eternity (Eph 1:4) and therefore not dependent "on human will or exertion" (Rom 9:16). The idea of election is a key issue in the Bible, but Augustine is the first among the church's teachers who puts it on the agenda and emphasizes its doctrinal significance.[2]

The doctrine of election invites rational objections. If Paul and Augustine are right that divine election cannot be understood as God's prescience about whether a human chooses to believe or not, what are the implications for the understanding of human freedom? If God's gracious

---

2. Hägglund, *History of Theology*, 133-42.

recreation of the human's attitude is the foundation of a trusting faith relationship, how can a loving God, who according to the apostle "desires all people to be saved" (1 Tim 2,4), seemingly let vast numbers of people remain indifferent or hostile? Attempting to give logically irrefutable answers to questions like these, one will soon find oneself caught by a net of contradictions. One should therefore rather remain with the conclusion from the Christological debates and admit that we here are confronted by problems we do not fully comprehend, and we may never do. Again, it seems to be advisable to find what we may clarify in a methodically consistent way and remain satisfied with that.

Augustine may not have entirely followed that principle, but it was the basics of his approach, and not Pelagius's objections, that became the generally accepted conclusion of the church. It was, for example, expressed through the decisions of the Council of Orange in Southern France in 529, about a hundred years after the death of Augustine.[3] There were both methodological and dogmatic reasons for the decision. When Pelagius reduces the understanding of sin to only include sinful *actions*, his position differs from what the New Testament has to say about this, and the death of Jesus as atonement for sin loses much of its significance. There are problematic aspects with Augustine's understanding of original sin. He sees it as transmitted from a generation to the next through sexual desire, which is an idea that is not found in the New Testament. However, there is no doubt that the New Testament considers sin a power that inevitably captures us, and from which we cannot liberate ourselves simply through a decision to be free. Consequently, the grace of God cannot be reduced to an announcement of where to find grace. It is a power for restructuring our lives and a mystery to be engulfed by. Appropriation of the gospel of grace is therefore not a procedure to be looked up in a book and then applied through a decision to live by its step-by-step requirements. It is a spiritual reality wherein we find ourselves and is to be maintained through the means that stand at our disposal. This is a doctrine of grace that may invite critique for not taking the obligation of obedience seriously. Both Jesus and Paul were met with this critique (Luke 7:34; 15:2; Rom 6:1). Both the apostles and Paul agree that this critique builds on a misunderstanding.

This understanding of grace has its costs. If salvation through grace alone implies that one has nothing to boast of before God (Eph 2:9), then the difference between the one who trusts God and the one who does not

---

3. Bettenson, *Documents of the Christian Church*, 66–68.

cannot be created by anything humans do. This creates a rational challenge closely related to the paradoxes of Christology. In both cases, we are confronted by the reality of God being present in the human context in a way that is real without being comprehensible by human logic. There is thus a connection between Arianism and Pelagianism. Not in the sense that Pelagius and his followers were Arians; they were not. There are, however, parallels in the attempt to logically control divine presence and divine revelation. The implication of Augustine's critique of Pelagius is that this should be seen to be as impossible in soteriology as it is in Christology. Divine presence is something one is confronted by, and one then has to live with the consequences one way or the other. By replacing this approach by a demand for rational understanding, one insists on the centrality and significance of one's own self in a way that is incompatible with the understanding of faith that is expressed both in the creeds and in Augustine's rejection of Pelagius.

The advantage of letting go of the objections and, on the faith journey, letting oneself be led where one did not intend to go, is that the parallel between human relationships of trust and the God-relationship becomes clear. Trusting relationships between humans are not governed by reason. Trust occurs spontaneously among persons who appear to be trustworthy. One cannot force oneself to trust a person who has proved to be unreliable. Christian faith comes into being by God appearing as trustworthy to us through the story about his Son. As with human relationships, we may not be able to answer all possible questions concerning the person we trust. However, presence is always presupposed. Trust will never be generated where there is no relation. To accept the spirituality of a life in faith as an existential challenge is therefore the precondition for a trusting God-relationship to be generated and nourished.

The doctrine of election as a problem of theological method

In the same way as two-nature Christology, the understanding of salvation as one-sidedly anchored in the grace of God has proved to be methodologically challenging. The influence of Augustine and the biblical foundation of large parts of his argument made it impossible for medieval theologians to return to the position of Pelagius. The understanding of sin as something more than the individual sinful acts and the atoning death of Jesus as a real victory over the power of sin was thus established as an inescapable framework for theological thought. However, the demand of the medieval university theologians for clarity and univocity even lead to a shift in the way one understood the God-relationship. One tried to mollify the paradoxes of the Pauline-Augustinian doctrine of election by introducing the idea of prevenient grace, according to which the grace of God surrounds humans in manifold ways before and independent of the establishment of a trusting relationship. Through prevenient grace, humans may take the first steps on the journey of faith, like attending worship service, listening to the word of God with interest, and trying to follow the divine commandments. Those who thus prepare themselves to the best of their ability will be met with saving grace, which through the salvific power of the sacraments will enable the human to do what God demands.[4]

When understood in this way, salvation becomes a three-step-model, where God performs both the first and the last step through prevenient and saving grace, but he is dependent on the human cooperation concerning step two for the process to succeed. This is called Semi-Pelagianism or synergism. In this way, one tried to maintain Augustine's understanding of the significance of grace without having to refer the difference between believers and unbelievers to something that seemed like arbitrariness and favoritism in God.

The problem was that divine salvation then always was dependent in humans being able to play their part. For those who are as good at analyzing themselves as Augustine and his most famous disciple, the Augustinian monk Martin Luther, this becomes a reason for anxiety ("*Anfechtung*" in Luther's German), as one can never trust oneself to have yielded what is demanded for God to do his part. Through his reading of the Bible and Augustine, Luther came to the conclusion that the rationalizing three-step-model was erroneous. If a text like Romans 8:28 ("for those who love God all things work together for good") is to be taken seriously, God must control the *entire* process, not only parts of it. This is also what the text says; they who love God are "called according to his purpose."

The critique of late medieval Semi-Pelagianism was thus the soil from which the Lutheran Reformation grew. Luther's point is the rather obvious one that grace, to remain grace and not drift in the direction of merit, must be *unconditional*. Grace founded on advantageous aspects of the graced one, is not grace, but merit. This was the foundation for Luther's work as a

---

4. Hägglund, *History of Theology*, 200.

theologian and teacher of the church; the rest of the Reformation was nothing but a realization of the necessary implications.

Luther early became aware that this emphasis on unconditioned grace placed him where both Jesus, the apostles, and Augustine had already arrived, i.e., in the understanding that a trusting God-relationship is established through a creative and elective act of God. He consistently maintains that this must be understood as an existential approach to the unknowable and unsearchable God, and that one therefore always errs in rearranging it as a logically unassailable thought construction. This is something he clarified primarily in his discussion with Erasmus of Rotterdam (1466–1536). Erasmus had two objections against Luther's radical understanding of divine grace. He thought it made humans morally lazy (that is essentially the same as Pelagius's objection against Augustine), and it seems that God arbitrarily elects persons for salvation or damnation. Therefore, Erasmus with the Semi-Pelagians maintained that there must be something in the human, primarily the honest desire to be a better person, that God appreciates in saving this person.

Luther rejected both objections. The first one he rejected by referring to the significance of spirituality. When humans are surrounded by the word of God, it effects a recreation of the person so that one starts to bring forth what Paul calls "the fruit of the Spirit." Luther was both a monk and a professor of theology. He thus had one foot in the monastic tradition and one in the scholarly tradition of the university. His aim as a Reformer was to unite the two to the effect that the monastic tradition was brought in contact with everyday life. Persons in ordinary jobs cannot attend prayer liturgies in the church seven times a day, as the monks and nuns did, but they can, as Luther emphasizes in the Catechisms, read their morning and evening prayers and say grace when eating. In this way, the believers remind themselves of the presence of God in which they "live and move" (Acts 17:28). The honest desire for becoming a better person is a good thing, but will in itself produce nothing but anxiety that the goal may not have been reached yet. A trusting God-relationship must have a different foundation, and the way that leads to this goal is to be surrounded by the creative power of the word of God through prayer and exposition to the Bible text.

Erasmus's second objection Luther rejected by saying that what God does or does not do is not for humans to evaluate. He here explicitly referred to the biblical idea of divine unknowability, which he found indispensable to avoid humans replacing the revelation of divine wisdom as the structuring principle of theology with their own rationality. In relation to God, we can only accept what we receive, not demand what he does not want to give (cf. Rom 9:20). The solution of the problem that originates in the conflict between God's gracious love and his judgment of unrepentant sinners is something we will have to leave for God to solve. Someday we may understand the solution, or we may not. To refrain from having the problem solved for us now is an important aspect of faith as trust.[5]

There is a close relation between Luther's Christologically anchored understanding of reality (cf. chapter 4b) and his rejection of all attempts to solve the problems of the doctrine of election. In both cases, his insistence on founding his understanding of reality in the infinity of God leads to rejecting the arranging of reality according to the presuppositions of human reason. Consequently, Luther can go quite far in accepting different theological statements without caring too much about logical consistency as long as the statements have a good biblical foundation. He here refers to the two-nature Christology of the Council of Chalcedon as a methodological example.[6] Applied on the humans' relationship to God, this amounts to letting the demands for obedience keep their significance as guiding principles to be taken seriously without drawing conclusions from the fulfilment or non-fulfilment of the commandments for the understanding of the reality of salvific grace. We shall love our neighbors and leave salvation to God. He is considerably better at it than we are.

For Luther, the human and the divine are parallel structures that both encompass all of life's realities while still being independent of each other. They do not affect each other as mutually dependent elements in a process, as Semi-Pelagianism will have it. The task of the human is to realize the truly human under all circumstances. The demand for perfection in the Sermon of the Mount (Matt 5:48) is not to be reduced to the level of the doable. The work of God is to place the human in the world by giving it life in its fullness, and to recreate the abandoned trust in God. Both are something God does without evaluating the moral or religious competence of humans. The parallel between the two structures are well summarized in Phil 2:12-13: "Work out your own salvation with fear and trembling, for it is God who works in you, both to will and to work for his good pleasure."

---

5. Alfsvåg, *What No Mind Has Conceived*, 239–50.

6. Steiger, *Communicatio Idiomatum as Axle and Motor*; Alfsvåg, *The Centrality of Christology*.

The Semi-Pelagian alternative implies a division of life between divine and human elements in a way that resembles both Nestorian Christology and the modern spiritualization of the God-relationship. In this way, the divine and the human are related to each other in ways that can be subjected to rational control, and the human remains in charge. The implication is an understanding that if I do like this (try to be a good person, use the sacraments of the church, etc.), God will do like that (give eternal life). This leads to an externalization of the God-relationship that might be more rational and thus more easily graspable. But is leads to a kind of spirituality that is quite far from what the New Testament, Augustine, and Luther are thinking of when they insist that the core of Christian spirituality is to experience the work of God (John 6:44, 65; Rom 9:16).

Luther is not dependent on explicating the doctrine of election to get this point through. In this respect, he resembles the Greek church fathers, who approach theology from the angle of Christology, but without explicitly discussing the doctrine of election. Maximus the Confessor (580–662) is a good example of this. He is a mystic who is concerned with the spiritual discipline needed for experiencing the soul's union with God. When this happens, however, this is always the result of a divine gift that does not depend on the quality of the preparation. The idea that this should be the effect of human merit is as strange to Maximus as it is to Luther.[7] However, Luther has his own boldness in relating this emphasis to the biblical texts on election.

Even Jean Calvin was concerned about the biblical and Augustinian doctrine of election as a rejection of Semi-Pelagianism. However, he does not relate the paradoxes of the doctrine election to divine unknowability in the way Luther does. Consequently, he has a more unambiguous understanding of election as God's eternal predestination of the ones who are to be saved and the ones who are to be condemned. He then manifests his power by letting his eternal decree become reality. This gives Reformed (Calvinist) theology its characteristic emphasis on God's glory.

Calvin's and his successors' strictness on this point caused a Semi-Pelagian reaction, which after its leader Jacobus Arminius (1560–1609) is called Arminianism. The Arminian understanding of the gospel as an offer of salvation that humans must decide to accept was taken over by Methodism and by and large by the English-language revival movements, including Pentecostalism. The understanding of reality then becomes more rational

---

7. Alfsvåg, *God's Fellow Workers*.

and less paradoxically ambiguous, and the understanding of the believer as recreated through God's grace less radical than in Augustine and Luther. In Pietism, we have a parallel development within Lutheranism.

Obedience and discipleship under modernity and postmodernity

Theology under the assumptions of modernity with its spiritualization of the God-relationship and the emphasis on the rationality of the independent human leads to an understanding of reality with strong elements of Pelagianism or Semi-Pelagianism. This affects both revival movements and Protestant university theology after the Enlightenment. Despite the starting point of the Reformation being the rejection of Semi-Pelagianism, one-sided Pelagianism has met with greater opposition from the Roman Catholic Church, though it has still not abandoned the kind of Semi-Pelagianism that it adopted at the Council of Trent (1545–63). This opposition seems to be due to the fact that a liturgical spirituality always has been important within Roman Catholicism. Consequently, Catholicism has, despite a certain resistance on the theory level, in practice followed Augustine's and Luther's insistence on immersion in divine wisdom as the most important methodological principle of both theology and a life in faith.

The great anti-Arminian exception in Protestant theology is Karl Barth, who shares Augustine's and the Reformers' understanding of the significance of the doctrine of election. However, Barth follows Calvin in rejecting divine unknowability as the framework of the doctrine of election. Here it seems that modernity's demand for unambiguity is accepted even by Barth. But he does not follow Calvin in understanding God's eternal election as a predestination of the elect and the cursed. Barth rather suggests that God has placed everybody under judgement to finally subject all to his mercy (cf. Rom 11:32: "God has consigned all to disobedience, that he may have mercy on all"). Barth thus moves in the direction of a doctrine that everybody eventually will be saved. This is understandable. Nobody is saved by pointing to an advantage in themselves. Considering oneself saved thus necessarily implies a hope and an expectation that this reality eventually will encompass everybody (cf. 1 Cor 13:7). This is an implication that is repeatedly referred to in the New Testament (Rom 14:11; Phil 2:10–11). At the same time, the believers are warned against being tempted into a false sense of security (Rom 11:20; 1 Cor 10:12). The texts informing us about the eternal judgment therefore remain, and nothing is withdrawn from their seriousness (Matt 10:28; 25:31-46; Rev 20:11-15). The tension between God's love, God's power, and God's judgment is not resolved. God is not subjected to rational unambiguity. We have therefore no reason to believe that the tensions of divine revelation will be resolved in ways we will understand. This respect for the logically ungraspable in God is more explicit in Augustine and Luther than in Calvin and Barth.

From the last part of the twentieth century, the philosophical school of postmodernity has criticized modernity's view of itself as the representative of progress and development. A precondition for postmodernity is Kuhn's critique of the idea that science always represents improvement. Another element of postmodernity is the recognition that technological progress is not always progress. On the contrary, is has given us problems with pollution and climate change. Faith in progress may thus be nothing but superstition.

Several postmodern thinkers have seen the connection between the critique of modernity and the paradoxes of the understanding of God. Jacques Derrida (1930-2004) has in his critique of modernity's demand for univocity focused on the unbridgeable difference between concept and phenomenon. The attempt at grasping reality by concepts is like running after the rainbow—when one comes to the place where one has seen it, it has always moved. This is essentially the same as the critique of a one-sided understanding of truth as correspondence between concept and reality, which I presented in chapter 2. Derrida explicitly relates this to the rejection of unambiguity in the understanding of God and reality in premodern theology and maintains that this gives a more adequate perception of reality than modernity's one-sided emphasis on rationality.

Derrida is still critical of what he calls messianism, which he understands as the tendency of religious traditions to re-establish unambiguity by pointing to the figure of a specific Savior. Even in relation to the Savior one should in Derrida's view retain the understanding of always arriving too late. In his view, every idea of the messianic creates an unfulfillable expectation. For Derrida, the important thing is the expectation of the unfulfillable, not the celebration of its realization.

The Roman Catholic theologian John Caputo (b. 1940) has employed Derrida' approach in a more explicitly theological context by asking us to listen for God's anonymous call. The call is unnamable and undefinable. No religious tradition can therefore have priority over against another. Instead of being concerned about rating each other, we should rather listen for the call to unlimited openness, hospitality, and care.

By bringing forth the skepsis of premodern theology toward definability as a criterion of reality, Derrida and Caputo have made us aware of the anthropocentrism that necessarily follows from modernity's demand for precision. In this way, they have shown the contradiction inherent in theological projects establishing themselves on the presuppositions of human rationality. On the other hand, one may doubt whether Derrida's and Caputo's rejection of modernity is as consistent as they think it is. When they reject the possibility of the realization of messianism and insists on the unending indefinability and anonymity of God's call, the skeptical human mind, which insists on its privilege to always postpone its judgement, remains at the center of the understanding of reality. As already Gregory of Nyssa insisted in his critique of Arius (chapter 4), taking divine infinity seriously implies accepting the possibility of divine self-manifestation, as one then cannot limit the possibilities of what God can do. This is, however, what Derrida and Caputo do when they reject the possibility of identifying God by means of a specific religious tradition. It therefore seems that Derrida and Caputo, despite their critique of modernity, remain within its anthropocentric limitations. Caputo has also been criticized for developing his position in an inconsistent way. If the call is infinitely indefinable, what is the reason for preferring hospitality and care before egoism and rejection?

The continuity between the premodern and the postmodern is maintained in a more consistent way by the Roman Catholic philosopher and theologian Jean-Luc Marion (b. 1946). He agrees with Derrida in his resistance against building the theological project on abstract concepts of reality. Except for mathematical concepts and concepts defined by natural science, our concepts never agree with reality. What is captured by precise concepts is but a small part of reality. There is always more to be said. That is the reason art always tries to express the ineffable. This is even more important when divine revelation is concerned. In this context, words are irreparably poor, as they always point to a reality that transcends their power of expression.

However, Marion does not remain in the ineffable. In the liturgical tradition of the church, mainly the Eucharist, God's reality breaks into our reality and encloses us in a divine fellowship. In this way, Marion retains the essential point that we can only relate adequately to God's infinite difference when we see his incarnational manifestation as a genuine reality. This is quite close to the way of thinking we find in Augustine and Luther.[8]

Divine wisdom as living water and theoretical knowledge

To summarize this chapter: We relate to the revelation of divine wisdom in two different ways. We can relate to it as a well within which we are immersed, paradigmatically in baptism, and later through the manifestations of divinity we are exposed to through a life in God's world. A biblical image of this reality is a stream of flowing water. Psalm 1 uses this as a description of an adequate God-relationship (Ps 1:1–3). Alternatively, we can relate to divine revelation as a communication of knowledge. Even this is a biblical idea (1 Cor 15:3–5).

These differing aspects of divine wisdom and its revelation must be held together. A one-sided emphasis on revelation as renewal without cognitive continuity leads to a spirituality void of content, which is often described as religious enthusiasm or *Schwärmerei*. A one-sided emphasis on revelation as communication of knowledge leads to a theoretical understanding of knowledge, which then may be analyzed logically and rationally. Then one will easily lose the living water imagery with its understanding of divine self-communication as what creates and shapes the human being in the context of both creation and recreation (salvation). When the recreated human being is understood as the work of God, one cannot at the same time think of it as an independent entity that can relate itself to divine revelation in a calculating and evaluative way. In the encounter between human possibility and divine creativity the believing and trusting subject comes (or does not come) into being. It is this point that Augustine and Luther try to capture by following the biblical authors in seeing election and recreation as the fundamental metaphors for this event. The path to renewal is to be exposed to the manifestation of divine wisdom, through which the believing subject is created. This implies that active participation in the liturgical life of the church is the one and only precondition for being an integrated theologian, and the one and only sign that you are one, because this is where the stream of living water is made manifest for us.

---

8. Alfsvåg, *Postmodern Epistemology and the Mission of the Church*.

A one-sided emphasis on the communication of knowledge tends to understand the human subject as essentially unchanged through this process, the implication of which is the one may consider oneself able to analyze it theoretically. This analysis can be performed in one of two ways. One can consider divine election as a reality, and human history will then be seen as a realization of a preconceived division of all humans in two groups. This is Calvin's solution. Or one can reject the doctrine of election for an understanding of divine revelation as an offer humans are free to accept or reject. This is the understanding of Semi-Pelagianism and Arminianism.

The implication of the latter solution is a spirituality where one tends to see exposure to the manifestation of divine wisdom as insufficient. It therefore must be completed with a warrant that the personal appropriation of this manifestation is real. The different aspects of the understanding and communication of divine wisdom then fall apart to the effect that the theory dimension and the experience dimension are isolated from each other. In the late medieval Semi-Pelagianism that Luther opposed, the experience dimension was isolated in the form of a penitential practice that among other things led to the trade in indulgences. In Protestant Semi-Pelagianism (Arminianism) one has focused on other faith expressions as signs that the faith decision of the believer is real. This led to the interest in Methodism and Pietism for specific acts or their absence as the sign of true faith (cf. the debate on the so-called adiaphora, like theatre, dancing, alcohol, etc.). In the Pentecostal revival movements, it is first and foremost speaking in tongues and miraculous healings that have been considered confirmation of faith's genuineness. One may be inclined to think that specific experiences in this way are given a significance they do not have in the New Testament. I will discuss this problem further in the chapter of the experiential dimension of theology (chapter 8).

The understanding of the manifestation of divine wisdom as real renewal is accompanied by the understanding that this is not something one is free to choose or not. By thinking of the human as a subject that freely chooses between religious alternatives one places oneself rather one-sidedly within the understanding of revelation as communication of knowledge. The image of living water does not work with freedom of choice, but with an understanding that what one is captured by and therefore lives by, will make itself know through the way one lives one's life.

SECOND PART
Sources of theological knowledge

6

The Bible as source and norm for Christian theology

The two parts of the Bible

THE FIRST FIVE CHAPTERS of this book have discussed the fundamental presuppositions for working with Christian theology: how do we get knowledge (chapter 2) about God (chapter 3) and God's revelation (chapter 4), and how one can become a theologian (chapter 5). An important conclusion is that this can only be done if the cognitive, existential, and liturgical aspects of theology are integrated in each other. In the second part of the book, I will discuss how we can relate to the different sources of theological knowledge in a way that maintains this integrated view of theology.[1]

The most significant feature of Christian worship across times and cultures is probably the reading and exposition of texts from the Bible as Holy Scripture. Worship services may be quite diverse, but there is at least one thing they have in common (with the sole exception of Quakers gathered for silent worship): there will be reading from the Bible, very often also a sermon on a biblical text.

This is sufficiently prominent to require an explanation. The fact that the Bible consists of two parts, the Old and the New Testament, even necessitates not only one, but two explanations. At the same time, this makes the relationship between the two parts a problem of its own. We are here confronted with the highly exceptional feature that two otherwise quite distinct faith traditions, the Jewish and the Christian, share the same Holy Scripture. They disagree, however, on the interpretation on the text they share, and this disagreement is mainly created by the text they do not share. How should these things be understood?

---

1. On this topic, see also McGrath, *Christian Theology: An Introduction*, chapter 6.

The Old Testament (which the Jews call the Tanakh) is the result of a long and complicated history we cannot discuss here. At the time of the events of New Testament, it already existed as a collection of holy writing with roughly the same content as the Old Testament we use today. Decisive for Christians' relation to the Old Testament was Jesus's attitude towards it. He repeatedly referred to the Old Testament, both to confirm its significance (cf. Matt 5:17) and to show that the deeds he performed were in accordance with the Old Testament prophecies about the coming Messiah (cf. Matt 11:5). Concerning the latter point, his Bible lecture for the two disciples on their way to Emmaus on the day of the resurrection seems particularly important (Luke 24:27, cf. v. 44). According to Jewish tradition, the Tanakh consists of three parts, the Law, the Prophets, and the Writings, and in this Bible lecture Jesus showed that it was the main point of all three to show how Messiah had to go through both suffering and death to new hope beyond death. What Jesus just had done was thus in accordance with the messianic pattern found in the Old Testament.

According to the Gospels, the disciples were quite slow in grasping the main points of the teaching of Jesus. But they got this point right, and from the day of Pentecost, their proclamation, particularly when directed to Jews, consisted in emphasizing that Jesus was the promised Messiah, and that his ministry corresponded to the pattern described in the Old Testament (Acts 2:22–26; 13:16–41). From the outset, it was thus the Old Testament that was the Holy Scripture of the church, and a Jesus-centered exposition of this collection of writings was the core of the Christian proclamation.

As the story is told the Gospels, Jesus added some measures to stabilize the communication of what he had said and done. He gave the disciples authority to proclaim that the messianic prophecies were fulfilled and instructed them concerning the significance of this fulfilment. Again, Luke 24 gives us the most detailed exposition: "Thus it is written, that the Christ should suffer and on the third day rise from the dead, and that repentance for the forgiveness of sins should be proclaimed in his name to all nations, beginning from Jerusalem. You are witnesses of these things" (vv. 46–48). The point is repeated in different ways in the other Gospels, cf. John 20:21–23: "Jesus said to them again, 'Peace be with you. As the Father has sent me, even so I am sending you.' And when he had said this, he breathed on them and said to them, 'Receive the Holy Spirit. If you forgive the sins of any, they are forgiven them; if you withhold forgiveness from any, it is withheld'" (John 20:21–23).

There are thus two aspects of the apostles' ministry, the proclamation of the message about Jesus to all peoples, and the maintenance of its authenticity. The apostles took both aspects seriously. They started their work as itinerant preachers. This is how the Acts of the Apostles describes the ministry of Peter and Paul. After a few years they started writing down their message, first in letters to the newly established congregations, later through the stories of the life of Jesus we know as the Gospels. It seems that the congregations soon started to read from the writings of the apostles in the worship service, as they did from the Old Testament writings. This tells us that these new writings were on their way to be seen as authoritative on par with the Old Testament. This process accelerated when the apostles died, and the congregations could no longer check the authenticity of the story of Jesus through the confirmation of the eyewitnesses. In this way, the New Testament came into being as a collection of the writings of the apostles and their closest collaborators. The precise content of the collection changed somewhat from congregation to congregation; uniformity in this respect does not seem to have been prioritized in the early church. However, the criteria for what could be accepted as an authoritative New Testament writing were quite stable. An authoritative New Testament writing should be written by an apostle or a close collaborator and should agree with the unanimously accepted central writings as far as doctrinal content was concerned. The central writings were the Gospels and the central Pauline letters.

In this way, the double canon of the church was established. Canon means rule or criterion for evaluation, and was the word used about the writings that mediated the presence of the risen one in an authentic way and therefore were used as holy writings and as the doctrinal norm of the church. These writings were read and explained in the worship service, and it was the meditation and reflection on what was written here that gave shape to a life in faith and obedience.

It was, however, not obvious how the two parts of the canon should be related to each other. There was extensive agreement that Jesus should be understood as the fulfilment of the messianic prophecies. This established a continuity between the Old and the New Testament, while the Messiah-texts of the Old Testament became essential for the understanding of the person and work of Jesus. This is, in the New Testament, summarized in the following way: you are "built on the foundation of the apostles [New Testament] and prophets [Old Testament], Christ Jesus himself being the cornerstone" (Eph

2:20). There was also agreement that one could find important examples of faith and ministry in the Old Testament. This is something the apostles and their co-workers emphasized in their preaching (cf. Heb 11), and it was both easy and edifying to find such examples. More problematic was the relationship to the law. Early on, the question was, did the Old Testament law apply even to gentile Christians? Later, one had to evaluate the view of people who had a critical attitude toward the Old Testament as a whole and thought it should be ejected from the Christian canon.

There are two types of Old Testament commandments: rules for worship (sacrificial laws, sabbatical laws, laws concerning circumcision) and rules for life (e.g., rules concerning compensation when one has accidentally hurt the livestock of the neighbor; Exod 21:35–36). Nobody seems to have considered the sacrificial laws a problem, as Jesus had brought the perfect sacrifice (cf. Heb 9:12). The termination of the sacrifices brought about by the destruction of the temple in 70 AD was thus much more of a problem for the Jews who did not believe in Jesus as the Messiah than it was for the Christian Jews, who could look to the sacrifice of Jesus. There were also morally relevant parts of the Old Testament law that were confirmed, in some cases even strengthened, by Jesus and the apostles in ways all Christians found to be decisive. This is the case both concerning affairs connected with what is usually called the fourth commandment (respect for parents; cf. Matt 15:4–6), the fifth (prohibition of murder; cf. Matt 5:21–22), and the sixth (prohibition of adultery; Matt 5:27–32; 1 Cor 6:15—7:40).[2] This was felt to be unproblematic, if not in practice, so at least in principle. However, the first generations of Christians struggled with other parts of the Mosaic law, in particular those related to circumcision and the rules for clean and unclean animals. This struggle was a continuation of the critique law-abiding Jews had directed towards what they considered as an unacceptable liberty from Jesus in relation to the law of Moses, particularly concerning the Sabbath commandment (Matt 12:1–15; cf. Gen 2:2–3 and Exod 20:8).

The discussion continued among the first generation of Christians. They struggled with the problem of circumcision, which according to the law shall be performed on Jewish boys when they are eight days old (Gen 17:12). This is still practiced by Jews. Peter and Paul included uncircumcised males in the congregations and were criticized for this. The

---

2. Some consider these commandments as the fifth, sixth, and seventh commandment, due to the fact that they see the prohibition of carved images as a separate commandment.

apostles met to discuss the problem and agreed that the two were right. The relationship with God is based on what Jesus has done, not the obedience toward specific commandments (Acts 15; see particularly vv. 9–11). Later Paul treated the question at length in Galatians. He had a radical solution. Jesus has fulfilled the ministry that includes humans in a trusting God-relationship. The Old Testament commandments regulating the relationship between God and humans can therefore only be considered provisional (Gal 3:23–24) or as figures of what now is realized—a main point in Hebrews. This also pertains to the two commandments that were older that the revelation of the law at Mount Sinai: The commandment to rest from work on the sixth day (cf. Col 2:16), and the commandment concerning circumcision. These commandments cannot by applied to Christians in their concrete form, even if Paul does not reject that they who are called as Jews may continue to live as Jews as long as the obedience to these commandments are not given a theological significance on par with the sacraments of the church (cf. 1 Cor 7:18).

Jesus summarized the law of Moses in the double commandment of love (Matt 22:37–40) but he is still critical toward a literal interpretation of the commandment to rest from all work on the Sabbath (Saturday). The obligation to do what is good is valid all days (Matt 12:12). He let the rest of the Decalogue remain as guidelines for the fulfilment of the commandment to love one's neighbor (Matt 19:18), though he obviously considered external obedience according to the letter of the commandment insufficient. Except for the Sabbath commandment, the Decalogue therefore remained in place as guidelines for the life of Christians (cf. 1 Tim 1:9–10, which gives an exposition of the Decalogue for Christians). Apart from this, the instructions of Jesus and the apostles for a life according to the will of God do not consider the specifics of the Old Testament law important. Christians should therefore see them as examples of obedience related to the context in which they originated.

Christians have not always been satisfied with this fairly liberal attitude toward the Old Testament commandments. We have hardly seen attempts at reintroducing circumcision for Christians, but other parts of Israel's laws have from time to time been considered important (e.g., Lev 12:1–7). Much of the discussion has centered on the attitude toward the Sabbath. Within the Reformed (Calvinist) tradition, there has been a tendency to transfer the Sabbath commandment to Sunday, and thus reinterpret the command to rest on Saturdays as a commandment to rest on Sundays. However, there is no support in the New Testament for this reinterpretation. The New Testament presupposes, but does not command, Sunday worship, as this was the day of the resurrection of Jesus (cf. Acts 20:7). Sunday, at the time, was neither a holiday nor a day of rest. This changed after the Constantinian reform in the fourth century, when everybody was supposed to attend the Sunday worship service. The fact that the resurrection of Jesus occurred on the first (or eighth) day of the week, was in the New Testament seen as the sign of the beginning of recreation (cf. 1 Cor 15:20). The New Testament does not connect the theology of the Sabbath to the resurrection of Jesus or to the celebration of worship on the first day of the week.

The attempt at seeing Old Testament commandments as valid today without considering their theological or social context is called biblicism. There is no similar problem regarding the New Testament exhortations concerning conduct and obedience. There are several reasons for that. In the period between the ascension and return of Jesus we are at the same level within the history of salvation. The teaching of the New Testament is therefore directly relevant for Christians in a way that cannot be presupposed for the Old Testament. In addition, the New Testament commandments are quite few and expressed in a way that is only loosely connected with the social context. Both the commandment to always love one's neighbor and the list of the fruits of the Spirit in Galatians 5:22–23 are valid in all contexts. The warnings against the dangers of wealth and against treating one's spouse thoughtlessly and egoistically have not lost their importance over the years.

There is thus both continuity and discontinuity in the relation between the two parts of the double canon of the church, and even the continuity created problems. The church was soon confronted by the challenge of Marcion (c. 85–c. 160). He rejected the revelation of the Old Testament law and the continuity between creation and salvation. According to Marcion, the world was not created by the loving God, the Father of Jesus, but by another deity, which he called the Demiurge. In this respect, he may have been influenced by Gnosticism (see chapter 4), but he also shows signs that he, like other parts of the early gentile church, could be overly critical of everything considered Jewish. For Marcion, the conclusion was clear: the Old Testament should not be a part of the canon of the church and should not be seen as Holy Scripture by Christians.[3]

---

3. Hägglund, *History of Theology*, 41–42.

THE BIBLE AS SOURCE AND NORM FOR CHRISTIAN THEOLOGY

The most important opponent of Marcion was Irenaeus of Lyon (c. 125–c. 203). He emphasized that the New Testament understands salvation as the restoration of the original and trusting relationship between God and human described in Genesis 2. This implies a continuity between creation and salvation, and thus even between the Creator and the Savior. Here Irenaeus follows the understanding of Jesus and the apostles. According to Jesus, Genesis 2:24 expresses the original, and still valid, will of God (Matt 19:4-6).

After the Enlightenment, a position close to Marcion's has resurfaced from time the time, e.g., in the German church historian Adolf von Harnack (1851–1930). Representatives of this view consider the Old Testament a collection of writings that primarily are interesting as sources for the political and religious history of the ancient Jews. In addition, one may be appalled by what is seen as the morally deficient parts of the Old Testament where God commands his people to wage holy war and realize a policy of extinction in relation to other nations (e.g., Num 21:3; Deut 2:23; 7:16; 13:15; Josh 6:21; 1 Sam 15:3). Abraham's descendants were elected to be a blessing, not a curse (Gen 12:3). How can exhortations to wars of conquest and killing of civilians belong in a collection of writings pretending to be a revelation from the loving God? In addition, the Old Testaments reflects a patriarchal society at variance with the revaluation of the position of women we have in the New Testament, e.g., in the teaching of Jesus about marriage and divorce.

As far as the latter point is concerned, however, Jesus maintains that what we have in the Old Testament is accommodation to the level of morality common at the time, not the original will of God (Matt 19:8). This is a point of view that might be relevant also in connection with the holy war-texts. Drastic measures may have been considered necessary to maintain the overall target of God's history with his people in the Old Testament. The people and its faith must at all costs be preserved in order that the promised Messiah could come from this people. The extermination of the alien peoples is therefore connected with the critique of idolatry that repeatedly is directed also against the chosen people. This implies an understanding of God as the Lord of history, even through war and disaster, that easily squares with his position as the Creator and Preserver of all there is, irrespective of its level of goodness, but it is difficult to align with the understanding of God as essentially determined by his love of all humans. We are again confronted by the fact that for us, it seems impossible to unite the seemingly unfathomable depths of God's inner tensions. If God's promises of salvation are at all believable, God must be the Lord of history, including its disasters. The Old Testament does not evade this paradox, but refrains from any attempt at solving the riddle.

Differing from the Old Testament, the New Testament rejects all ideas of holy war. Jesus explicitly protests against being defended with violence (Matt 26:52–54; John 18:11). The final judgment of God's opponents will have to wait for the judgement on the last day. It shall, therefore, not be implemented now (Matt 13:30, 40–41). Metaphors of war are therefore in the New Testament only used in connection with spiritual warfare (Eph 6:11–17), and the use of violence is limited to the political authorities' punishment of evil (Rom 13:4). The recruitment of disciples should only be done through baptism and instruction (Matt 28:19–20), never coercion. Marcion and von Harnack are right that there is, in this respect, a marked difference between the Old and New Testaments, but this does not justify their overruling of Jesus by banning the Old Testament from the canon. In important aspects, though not in all aspects, there is thus continuity between the battles that are fought by the believers in the Old and New Testaments. It is essential to retain this continuity.

We must therefore keep the double canon of the church. Jesus is the fulfilment of the Old Testament promises, and the goal of his ministry is to restore the relationship with God that was established when God created the human in his image, a relationship that in the meantime has remained more or less unrealized.

The clarity of the Scripture and historical-critical Bible research

The biblical authors did not primarily intend to communicate knowledge concerning historical events, but to transmit the actual significance of divine revelation. This is something we see already in the Old Testament, where the story of the exodus from Egypt is given in the shape of a liturgy in which the events are recapitulated in order that those who are involved shall understand what this *means* for them (Exod 12; see particularly vv. 26–27). The same principle is applied to the retelling of the Old Testament history in the New Testament (1 Cor 10:6), and for the liturgical representation of the salvific events of the story of the New Testament (1 Cor 10:16).

This implies an understanding according to which there are layers in the texts, where the historical layer is primarily related to the person and work of Jesus—this holds even for the Old Testament texts—and the tropological or actualizing layer is related to the texts' meaning for us, serving as a mediator of divine presence to us. The actualizing aspects were gradually differentiated to the extent that one distinguished between the dogmatical or typological, moral, and anagogical (eschatological) applications. This is called the doctrine of the fourfold meaning of the Bible (Quadriga). The method could be used in ways we would consider arbitrary. However, the intention was to maintain the actual significance of the texts as interpretations of important aspects of the lives of the readers and listeners. At the same time, they knew that when dogmatic precision was concerned, they would have to refer to the historical-Christocentric interpretation. This is emphasized by Augustine, for instance.[4]

In the late Middle Ages, this pattern dissolves. The text's reference is then seen as the historical reality behind the text, which the interpreter wants to know as precisely as possible. The fellowship of the present readers of the text are then no longer parts of the story, and we get other models for actualizing the biblical doctrines.[5] This shift in the pattern of interpretation is closely related to the synergism that the Reformers reacted against. To fight this synergism, Luther returned to the original division between the historical-Christological and the tropological meaning of the text. The overall goal of the Bible is to represent the person and work of Jesus in such a way that we are included in the story it tells. What we often call Luther's reformatory discovery is by Luther himself presented as a discovery of how God, through the texts of the Bible, gives his justice as the reader's own reality: "Lead me, O LORD, in your righteousness" (Ps 5:8).

The significance of this discovery is clarified in Luther's discussion with Erasmus (cf. chapter 5). Erasmus maintains that the text of the Bible is a complicated text whose meaning is unclear. We therefore need an authoritative interpreter (the hierarchy) who can tell us what it means. Luther rejects this view by referring to the illuminative power of the biblical metaphors: "Your word is a lamp to my feet and a light to my path" (Ps 119:105). We must let go of the anxious worries of reason and let the text and its renewing potential lead us where it wants. As the central event in the biblical story is the resurrection of Jesus, the biblical text primarily manifests

---

4. Ayres, *Patristic and Medieval Theologies of Scripture*.
5. Hahn and Wiker, *Politicizing the Bible*, 54–55.

the presence of the risen one. Details may still by unclear, partly because we do not understand all linguistic and historical aspects of the text. However, we do not need to worry about that, as there is no need to remain in doubt concerning the overall meaning of the biblical story.

Through the text of the Bible The Holy Spirit manifests divine presence, which creates and sustains faith in the hearts of the humans. The relevant method for being captured and governed by the recreative power of the Spirit is therefore semantic and grammatical analysis of the text. One should primarily study the text in its original languages, as it opens access to the source, lessening the power of later interpretations that necessarily have influenced the translations. Luther distinguishes between the external clarity, which is proclamation as actualizing exposition of the biblical text, and inner clarity, which is the conviction of the heart. They are closely related. The inner clarity is created by the external, which is grasped by means of the inner. This is circular reasoning, which it must be; if not, the creative work of God in the human will not be seen as faith's foundation (cf. chapter 5). However, it is only the external clarity that is relevant for the congregation. A subjective conviction (inner clarity) is important for the individual having it, but the public proclamation of the church must always be a Christ-centered, grammatically and semantically precise exposition of the biblical text.

Luther, like the church fathers before him, is here influenced by an incarnational understanding of reality (cf. chapter 5). The Son of God has become a human and has communicated divine revelation through human words. Linguistic metaphors contain the possibility of saying what cannot be said; in Luther's view, this is the reason human words can communicate divine realities. In their direct and concrete meaning, words can never communicate anything but internal relations within the created world. We know what a lamb is; the Lamb of God, however, is something different (John 1:29). The meaning of words may be expanded to include the incarnational reality. That is the reason Jesus used parables; he wanted his audience to see something beyond the immediate reference of the words.

An interesting aspect of the understanding of the Bible, both in the early church and in Luther, is that they were not very interested in defining the extent of the biblical canon. The criteria for canonicity are important, but their application is determined through the use of the different writings in the church. The authority of the Bible is its message, and the significance of the text is determined by its use as manifestation of divine presence. The formal authority of the Bible (the canon as norm for doctrine and life) and its material authority (the text as manifestation of the presence of the risen one) merge.[6]

At the time of the Reformation, however, this untroubled identification of the formal and material authority of the Bible started to disintegrate. Both the counter-reformational Council of Trent and the Confessions of the Reformed Church contain lists of the books that belong in the Bible. The idea is thus that one first will have to establish the authoritative text, and then start interpreting it to grasp what it says. One has started distinguishing between (textual) fact and interpretation. This tendency was much strengthened from the time the Enlightenment when the fledgling historical interpretation began to see the biblical texts primarily as historical sources. Thus were introduced the two levels of interpretation characteristic of Protestantism under modernity. *First* comes the attempt at reconstructing the historical events behind the texts as we have them. One tries to discover the religious, literary, and political development for which the Old Testament texts are the most important sources, and in the same way one tries to find the realities of the life of Jesus behind the biased and proclamatory presentation in the Gospels. *Then* the truths of the reconstructed history should be applied to the contemporary situation to find their relevance for faith and life today. While the premodern interpretation of the Bible was primarily interested in retelling the biblical story as a story that included the contemporary readers and listeners, one now thinks that the goal of the academic work with the Bible is to distinguish between fact and fantasy in the texts, and in a subsequent process apply what can be gathered from the distilled facts as guidelines for the believers.[7]

With the benefit of hindsight, it is not too difficult to see what happened here. The modern preference for fact-based knowledge (cf. chapter 3) is applied to texts from the past, including the biblical texts. In the same way as in the natural sciences, this leads to an enormous growth of knowledge. As far as the Bible is concerned, the historical approach has vastly expanded our knowledge of linguistic, literary, and historical phenomena in the Middle East in biblical times. This expansion of knowledge comes at a price, though. All earlier generations had read the Bible primarily to find themselves explained by what they read. This was now considered a naïve and unacademic way of reading the Bible. Still, it did

---

6. Alfsvåg, *These Things Took Place as Examples for Us*.
7. Frei, *The Eclipse of Biblical Narrative*.

not die, but was retained by the liturgies of the church, which always have read the Bible in this way, and in the spiritually edifying Bible reading of believers. This created the tension between academic theology and everyday church life that has been a dominating feature of many Protestant churches since the Enlightenment.

One therefore needed theologians who could apply the new Bible hermeneutics in ways that were constructive for life in the church. This need was satisfied by Friedrich Schleiermacher (1768–1834), often called the church father of the nineteenth century. He developed a hermeneutics for the interpretation of historical texts, according to which he saw it as essential to grasp the distinctive character of former eras and their texts and submerge oneself in them. The aim was to grasp the past in its distinctive difference from the present, and from that starting point reconstruct the thought world of the people of the past as precisely as possible. Working with persons of the past, one should thus try to disregard what one's contemporaries would take for granted.

However, even Schleiermacher thought there were aspects of persons' attitudes that were stable over time. Here he was particularly interested in humans' feeling of dependence over against the transcendent. He then united the two perspectives and showed how distinctive features of texts of the past could be understood as realizations of humans' timeless religious needs. In this way, he could use historically reconstructed aspects of the biblical texts, e.g., expressions of confidence toward God in the Psalms or Paul's doctrine of justification, as attempts at making sense of one's situation in the world that were meaningful even in a contemporary perspective.

Schleiermacher thus succeeded in demonstrating that there was no necessary opposition between a historically informed interpretation of the biblical texts and their edifying application, and this made him highly influential. One proof of his significance is the fact that, from his model of interpretation, he developed the distinction between historical, philosophical (or systematic), and practical disciplines within which academic theology still works. The historical disciplines (the study of the Bible and church history) establish the historical facts, the philosophical-systematic analysis discusses the significance of these facts within a model of the context-transcending aspects of human existence, and the practical disciplines make use of this analysis for the benefit of everyday church life. The difference over against premodern Bible interpretation is primarily seen in the new recognition of our distance from the worldview that is reflected in the biblical texts. That worldview is not our worldview. Central aspects of the interpretation of reality we find in the biblical texts must therefore be translated to our way of thinking before they can be relevant for us.

This triad of historical knowledge, philosophical analysis, and practical application is characteristic of Protestant theology in the nineteenth and much of the twentieth century. The philosophical dialogue partners have over the past two centuries changed a lot, and with them the content of both analysis and application, but the model itself has been surprisingly stable.

It has, however, also met with heavy criticism. Three objections have been particularly important. Some scholars have rejected the basic presupposition, the difference between text and historical reality that makes the historical-critical analysis possible. For a long time, this was the case with the Roman Catholic Church, as Protestant Bible criticism was found to be lacking in several aspects. This objection disappeared during the twentieth century, though, and Protestant and Roman Catholic Bible scholars now cooperate from similar methodological presuppositions. The opposition from so-called fundamentalism has been less flexible. According to this approach, there is identity between text and historical reality as far as the Bible is concerned. Fundamentalists therefore insist that the Bible is infallible as regards the historical facts of its texts.[8] In this way, one aims at re-establishing the continuity with premodern Bible interpretation. However, this attempt does not succeed. Even fundamentalism differs from premodern scholarship by accepting the dichotomy between fact and interpretation, even if it claims to have an alternative access to the facts. A reconstruction of the facts of the past, infallible or not, is something distinctly different from the approach to the text as the manifestation of the reality of divine presence. Fundamentalism is thus captured by the philosophical presuppositions of modernity in the same way as the historical-critical approach.

More interesting is the critique of the historical reconstructions for being insufficiently self-critical. In the nineteenth century, one tried to reconstruct the life of Jesus from the presupposition that his God consciousness was the exemplary aspect of his life. In 1913, Albert Schweitzer (1875–1965) published the book *The Quest of the Historical Jesus*.[9] Here he showed how the scholars' understanding of Jesus was a projection of their

---

8. Farnell, *Vital Issues in the Inerrancy Debate*.

9. Schweitzer, *The Quest of the Historical Jesus*. The book was first published in 1906, but with another title.

own ideals and worldviews. The results of the research of the life of Jesus had little to do with the historical Jesus and quite a lot with the scholars' own assumptions. The critique was devastating, and the scholarly work intent at reconstructing the biography of Jesus was terminated. It has later been renewed with other methods and has grown into a complicated enterprise with quite diverse presuppositions and conclusions. The critique that this kind of historical research to a large extent is governed by the assumptions of the scholars, however, is still both strong and relevant. A similar critique has been directed against the attempted reconstructions of the history of Ancient Israel.

The third form of criticism is the one raised by Karl Barth and his disciples (cf. chapter 5). He thought that both Schleiermacher and other Protestant schools of theology made themselves too dependent on the dialogue with contemporary philosophy, resulting in an unclear compromise between the message of the Bible and what was commonly accepted among the scholars' contemporaries. In Barth's view, theology should aim at nothing less than the communication of a message from God. In doing so, one should not look left and right to see how this should be done in a way that ensured its relevance according to the criteria of contemporary culture. When God has spoken, humans should shut up and listen, not convey the message by negotiating with it.

Barth did not reject historical Bible research in principle, but did not pay much attention to it in practice. At least, that was the contention of Barth's critics. As a result of Barth's skepticism towards considering humanity's religious and moral sentiments a relevant negotiating partner, he has also been criticized for overlooking the importance of working with the conditions of an adequate epistemology. Theology may be working with revelation, the source of which is God's own reality, but it still has to be communicated by humans, and for Barth this tends to be a problem. Even Barth, then, may not quite grasp the paradoxical reality of divine presence communicated through human words and human witnesses. He will accept no compromise concerning the necessity of adequate theology being anchored in divine revelation; the outcome, however, is a certain vagueness in the understanding of how this kind of theology is communicated. Can we really trust that we receive the word of God from the human preacher on a Sunday morning? From Barth's suppositions, this is not a question that is easily answered.

The significance of the Bible after modernity

Both fundamentalism's inerrancy doctrine, Schweitzer's critique of the prejudiced use of sources, and Barth's critique of the adequacy of nineteenth-century Protestant theology point us to relevant elements, but none of them give us a satisfactory alternative to modern, Protestant biblical scholarship. An alternative has, however, been suggested by philosophical hermeneutics. In 1960, Hans-Georg Gadamer (1900–2002) published *Truth and Method*.[10] Here he showed how the reconstruction hermeneutics of Schleiermacher and Wilhelm Dilthey (1833–1911) was built on an unstable foundation. According to Gadamer, it is never possible to reconstruct the thought world of humans of the past. The basic distinction between fact and interpretation upon which modern historical scholarship, including historical-critical research of the Bible, has been built is unsustainable. When we approach classic texts from the history of religion or literature, we do that from presuppositions created by our own history. Gadamer calls these presuppositions prejudice, but he does not use that word in a negative sense. We are never fully aware of our own prejudice; neither can we fully liberate ourselves from them. But we utilize them when we ask questions to the texts we read. These texts have their own horizons, which are their own meanings in their original linguistic, literary, and historical context. In a similar way, the interpreter has his or her horizon, given with the baggage with which the text is approached. These are general and unalterable epistemic conditions.

Understanding is what occurs when the horizons of the text and the interpreter fuse as the interpreter grasps how the text makes sense within his or her own context. Two readers will never approach the text with the same prejudice and the same horizon. Their interpretations will therefore never be identical. A certain plurality of interpretations is therefore both necessary and desirable. However, not all interpretations are equal; there will always be interpretations that are better than others in the sense that they grasp the horizon of the text and thus its significance in a more meaningful way. But there is no single given and correct way of reading the text, and we will never have the definite interpretation.

There are certain similarities between Gadamer's emphasis on the significance of prejudice and Kuhn's emphasis that understanding always occurs within the context of a paradigm. At the same time, Gadamer

---

10. On which, see Zimmermann, *Hermeneutics: A Very Short Introduction*.

represents a return to some of the principles that governed the premodern Bible interpretation. Neither maintains a distinction between fact and interpretation, or between understanding and application; one has not understood the text until its message is applied in the life of the reader. The interpretation of the text thus aims at the understanding of its message in its actual significance, not at reconstructing the history behind the text. Our approach to art is therefore a better analogy with the interpretation of texts than the work of historians with their sources. We already have seen this idea in the work of Marcion (chapter 5).

This is a kind of hermeneutics that is open toward—and probably also inspired by—the possibility of textual interpretation as mediation of divine presence. In Europe, the history of hermeneutics is to a large extent the history of the principles of Bible interpretation. However, Gadamer is primarily interested in hermeneutics as a general aspect of the human production of knowledge. In this way, he solves the problem that for Barth remained unsolved. For Gadamer, it is not a problem, but a necessity that the actualizing application of the text's message is done by humans and with regard to the life of humans. This is the *only* way to achieve a humanly relevant fusion of horizons.

Even premodern biblical interpretation encouraged a certain plurality in the readings of the texts. There are principles of interpretation that are fairly stable, and the Christological debates of the early church were to large extent concerned with the question of finding and defining some of these principles of interpretation. Apart from that, one had no problem with accepting a quite extensive plurality of interpretations. This openness for interpretative plurality has remained with the church to this day, as two preachers may on the same Sunday interpret a given text in differing ways without anybody considering that a problem. The one-sided concentration on finding *the* correct interpretation of a set of given facts, which we have both under Protestant orthodoxy and under modernity, albeit in slightly different ways, is an aberration. Without undermining the incarnational mediation of divine presence as the overall aim of biblical interpretation, the reading of the Bible will have to be as manifold as life itself.

The discussion of method in Bible interpretation is today quite diverse. Some scholars still investigate the texts primarily as historical sources. Others, inspired by Gadamer and others in the same tradition, work with methods gathered from the study of literature to grasp the structure and meaning of the text. Some of these focus quite one-sidedly on what Gadamer called prejudice, i.e., what the reader brings to text, and consider interpretation as something the reader produces relatively independent from the text. Others again think that Gadamer does not pay sufficient attention to the reader's political and social context, and therefore maintain that his approach should be supplemented with perspectives that emphasize the text's potential for liberation from oppressive structures.

To find a way through this methodological plurality in a way that lets one work with the biblical text as mediation of divine presence is no easy task. However, Gadamer's text-oriented hermeneutics helps us in finding our way back towards an essential perspective from premodern biblical interpretation. It is the presentation of Jesus *in* the biblical texts that is the source of and norm for faith, not a reconstructed Jesus *behind* the text. The point is to believe as the apostles, not make one's own Jesus (Acts 2:42). At the same time, one should pay attention to the canonical wholeness within which the texts are communicated to us. The biblical texts are collected for a purpose: They will give us Jesus as the living Lord today. All that is helpful toward the realization of this goal is something Christian theology can apply with confident boldness. The empty tomb sets the perspective that gives everything its proper place. This does not entail the rejection of alternative approaches. To read the Bible as a collection of historical sources may produce knowledge that at least is indirectly relevant even for theology understood as actualized Bible interpretation. But it is the risen one and the encounter with him that establishes the overarching goal for the work with the Bible in Christian theology.

7

The history and unity of the church

The catholicity of the church

WE ARE NOT THE first Bible readers. The history of the church is to a large extent the history of the interpretation of the Bible, and the church has also as a fellowship repeatedly stated how the Bible should be understood. The history of the church and her interpretation of the Bible is therefore an important part of theology's collection of sources. What is the status of the history of the church in this connection?

According to the Gospels, the church was not established by coincidence. On the contrary, we are told that it was an important goal for Jesus to build a fellowship of believers he called church (Matt 16:18; in Greek *ekklēsía*). This fellowship, which gathers "in the name of Jesus," is something Jesus promises to take part in (Matt 18:20) and to preserve (Matt 28:20). In virtue of the death and resurrection of Jesus there is only one way to God. There is therefore only one fellowship of believers, even if they gather in different places and in different ways. As long as we speak about the church, the essentials are common for all believers: "One body and one Spirit, . . . one Lord, one faith, one baptism, one God and Father of all, who is over all and through all and in all" (Eph 4:4–6).

To maintain the unity of the church, there are specific demands that should be met, both concerning the way the message is communicated and concerning its content. The demands concerning the way of communication were clarified during the struggle with Gnosticism (cf. chapter 4). The gnostics based their doctrine on the existence of a secret, oral tradition for the inner circle of disciples. However, this distinction between ordinary disciples and an inner circle of privileged disciples is incompatible with the New Testament understanding of the unity and fellowship of the church. Through the rejection of Gnosticism, it was thus clarified that the communication of the

Christian message must be founded on open sources administered by a recognizable leadership in ways that are transparent and open to critique. These principles were implemented through the canonization of the New Testament and the communication of the message through an identifiable line of bishops who met from time to time to clarify the message of the church over against new challenges. The principles were codified by Irenaeus' refutation of Gnosticism in the second century (chapter 6) and continued through the great councils from the fourth century onwards.

The demands concerning an authentic communication of the content of the Christian message were in the fifth century explicated by Vincent of Lérins (d. about 450) in a way that has remained as a point of orientation in the debate on the unity of the church. He maintained that the most important sign of the catholicity of the church was to maintain the faith that has been believed "everywhere, always, and by all."[1] This can be understood as a specification of what the creeds aim at when they state that the church is catholic, which both the Apostles' and the Nicene Creed do. To be catholic means to believe in the one God, the one Savior, and the one way to salvation in accordance with the apostles and the entire Christian church. There is thus no room for minority positions or group formations. Everybody should have a sense of general obligation toward the fellowship of believers, and thus toward the common faith. Already in Paul we find critique of groups in the church that destroy the unity (1 Cor 11:19). "Group" in Greek is *haíresis*, and that is the origin of the world heresy, which is used for doctrines that divide by establishing their own rules for the unity of the church. The point is not that everybody must understand and agree on everything, or that everything must be done in the same way everywhere, but that one should not establish criteria for unity that differ from what traditionally and generally has been accepted as the essence of faith.

From the fifth century, it was for all practical purposes the Nicene Creed that served as the standard for unity and catholicity. To belong to the one, universal church was to confess the faith according to the Nicene Creed, which defined the faith over against important theological challenges in a way that was generally accepted. One of the signs of the position of this creed is that church councils for more than thousand years explicitly refer to the Nicene Creed as the foundation upon which they stand. The creed does not explain everything, and not all theological problems can be solved by just referring to what is said here. But it defines the essentials of

---

1. Hägglund, *History of Theology*, 144.

the authentic Christian faith, both concerning content and method. The document was primarily developed to refute the Arian misunderstanding concerning Trinity and incarnation, but it states some additional criteria for catholicity: the understanding of creation as a rejection of Gnosticism, the salvation of humans as the goal of the incarnation, and an explicitly sacramental understanding of baptism and the church as the area of the work of the Holy Spirit as life-giver and creator of faith.

The last document from the undivided church of Western Europe to explicitly refer to the Nicene Creed as the foundation of its own authority is the most important confessional document from the Lutheran Reformation, the Augsburg Confession or Confessio Augustana (hereafter referred to as CA), written in 1530. Read from within the context where it was written, this is not the creed of a particular denomination, but an attempt to confess the catholic faith according to criteria for unity taken from the Nicene Creed. CA consists of two parts. The first part, articles 1 through 21, presents the catholic faith as believed and practiced in the Lutheran congregations. The emphasis is here on agreement with the Nicene Creed (and the Council of Chalcedon), and with the rejections of heresy laid down by the Catholic Church through her history concerning the doctrine of the Trinity (article 1), the understanding of sin (articles 2 and 20; rejection of Pelagianism), the understanding of revelation (article 5), the understanding of the church (article 8), the understanding of sacrament and penitence (articles 9, 10, 12 and 13), the importance of civil ordinances (article 16) and eschatology (article 17).[2] Through the history it had been necessary to restate the understanding of faith in the Nicene Creed in a more precise way, but there are no gaps in the continuity of the communication of faith from one generation to the next. The Augsburg Confession considers itself a part of this continuity. It therefore presents itself as a confession of faith from the undivided Western Church, wanting to emphasize one point only. The Lutheran reform movement is catholic according to the understanding of Vincent and the Nicene Creed, and proves it by confessing the Christian faith in accordance with the Nicene Creed, and by being a part of the Catholic Church in rejecting all heresies that had abandoned catholicity by not accepting what had been believed "everywhere, always, and by all."

The second part of CA applies this principle of catholicity in a more polemical way. This part looks at positions and practices that at the time were relatively new, and therefore cannot be considered elements of the

---

2. Kolb and Wengert, *The Book of Concord*, 36–59.

church's catholicity; this has not been believed "everywhere, always, and by all." These practices may in themselves not be erroneous, but they become heretical when seen as conditions for church unity. Examples are the withholding of the chalice from lay Christians, the necessity of celibacy for all priests, and specific regulations of fasting. Both fasting and celibacy can under appropriate circumstances be good and commendable but are not acceptable as criteria for church unity.[3]

Challenged by the understanding of catholicity in the Augsburg Confession, the unity of the church in Western Europe collapsed, and it has not been restored yet. The Roman Catholic Church concluded that it had to reject the Lutheran reform movement as itself heretical. To do that, the Roman Catholic Church had to abandon the traditional understanding of catholicity and redefine it. For the Council of Trent, which redefined the Roman Catholic Church after the encounter with the Lutheran challenge, catholicity was no longer defined in accordance with that all believers had always believed. Catholicity was now to believe in accordance with what was decided by the Roman Catholic magisterium, be it pope or council. To defend this principle, one accepted the idea of "unwritten traditions" of doctrine besides and independent of biblical interpretation, and the two were to be venerated "with an equal affection of piety and reverence."[4] The council thus gave itself considerable liberty in defining doctrine without paying much attention to the principle of doctrinal continuity, and this was a liberty the council was not shy of using. The new principle of authority, equality between Scripture and the unwritten traditions, was itself a breach with tradition; no council had ever said anything like this before.

However, even among those who followed Luther in demanding ecclesial reform, there were many who did not accept the traditional understanding of the church's catholicity. Even in this camp, quite a few gave themselves considerable liberty in relation to church doctrine as communicated and received through the centuries. Many rejected the traditional liturgy and redefined the doctrine of the sacraments, no longer understanding the Lord's Supper as a manifestation of the presence of Jesus, but as a meal to commemorate the death of Jesus and its significance for believers. This was the position of Zwingli (cf. chapter 4). There were also those who were skeptical toward the baptism of children, which they saw as the reason for the existence of church members without real faith. They thought it better to postpone

---

3. Kolb and Wengert, *The Book of Concord*, 60-105.
4. Council of Trent, fourth session; Schaff, *The Creeds of Christendom*, 2, 80.

baptism until there was a conscious confession of faith in Jesus from the one to be baptized. Among these, some took one further step and found the baptism of children, which necessarily is performed upon the confession of faith from parents and sponsors, to be invalid. They therefore started to baptize anew those who had been baptized as children.

The Lutheran refutation of the argument of the Anabaptists is interesting, as it clearly shows the Lutheran Reformers' understanding of the church's catholicity. In refuting anabaptism, they did not refer to the Bible—there are no texts in the New Testament that explicitly address the question of children's baptism. They referred to the unambiguity of tradition. The church has always baptized the children of Christian families, and this has never been controversial. There is thus no doubt that baptism of children corresponds to Vincent's understanding of catholicity. For this understanding of catholicity, however, one could give biblical arguments. Jesus had promised that he would protect his church to the extent that "the gates of hell shall not prevail against it" (Matt 16:18; cf. 28:20: "I am with you always, to the end of the age"). If the administration of something as basic for church life as the sacrament of baptism has been erroneous throughout the entire history of the church, Jesus has not kept this promise. If, on the contrary, one accepts that Jesus has kept his promise, the entire church cannot have been in error concerning a doctrine as central as this one. To maintain this continuity is of utmost importance. Faith is nothing if not faith in the trustworthiness of the divine promises. For that reason, we are not at liberty to redefine the doctrine of the church in ways that ignore the historical realities of the communication of doctrine through the centuries.

The division of the church at the time of the Reformation was caused by the until then relatively uniform understanding of catholicity falling apart in three different models. 1) The insistence that an adequate understanding of the unity of the church implies real commitment to the principle of the continuity of the communication of doctrine. 2) The understanding that the hierarchy of the church under the guidance of the Spirit has the authority to define new doctrines independent of Scripture and the continuity of the communication of doctrine. 3) The understanding that continuity is unimportant if one has a biblical foundation for what is done.[5] Variation of the latter position is found among the Reformed and the Anabaptists.

5. Mathison, *The Shape of Sola Scriptura*, calls my position 1) tradition 1, position 2) is tradition 2, and position 3) is tradition 0, adding the later doctrine of papal infallibility as tradition 3.

It is often related to a kind of biblicism that indiscriminately maintains the validity of biblical commandments (cf. chapter 6). One sign of one's belonging to this tradition is the rejection of the traditional worship liturgy, replacing it with what is found to be in accordance with explicit New Testament commandments concerning the worship service.

Even before the time of the Reformation the church was divided in the Western, Latin, Roman Catholic part and the Eastern, Greek Orthodox part. There is considerably affinity between the understanding of catholicity in the Augsburg Confession and in the Orthodox Church. Both consider the Nicene Creed fundamental, and both find two-nature Christology to be the foundation of the understanding of salvation and the church. The Orthodox Church has always rejected the idea that the bishop of Rome (the pope) should be the head of the church—this is in itself an important reason the office of the pope cannot be catholic in the creed's sense. The Lutherans found this to be a fellowship in theology that was worthy of closer inspection, and there was already in the sixteenth century contact between the theologians in Wittenberg and the patriarch of Constantinople. However, the contact led nowhere. The churches in Western and Eastern Europe did not have much common history and therefore lacked a common language for the discussion of theological problems. This led to numerous misunderstandings, and to insurmountable problems even in defining the decisive questions. In spite of the disagreement with Roman Catholics being considerably more profound, it was easier discussing with them. Roman Catholics and Lutherans at least agreed on their disagreements.

The division of the church created a theologically challenging situation. The historical churches (Greek Orthodox, Roman Catholic, Lutheran, Anglican, Reformed) and many of the newer (Baptist, Methodist, Pentecostal) agree on the basic content of the Christian faith (incarnation and Trinity) and on the fundamental principles of its interpretation and communication. In spite of this, they draw differing conclusions concerning the criteria for unity to the extent that they work as separately organized ecclesial communities that in many cases cannot gather around the same table to receive the Eucharist together. Consequently, even the academic discipline of theology is divided in denominationally oriented schools that in some cases appear as different paradigms in a Kuhnian way. For churches that agree on the significance of a doctrinal statement as ambitious and precise as the Nicene Creed, should not this be a problem that could be solved?

The plurality of doctrine and the ecumenical movement

After the Reformation, the churches for a long time seemed satisfied with digging their different trenches from where they could refine their own views on the way to church unity. Unsurprisingly, this did not produce much growth in unity. This is not the situation today. Since the Enlightenment, there has been considerable movement across the trenches. However, these movements go in two different directions, and have therefore not succeeded in re-establishing the lost unity.

Protestant theology has to a large extent worked according a Reformed understanding of doctrinal tradition, finding it relatively unimportant. This has even included most Lutherans, both in the academy and in the revival movements. This in turn led to a plurality of models for theological normativity and did not contribute to the growth of unity.

In this respect, the ecumenical movement has been considerably more important. The origin of this movement was the experience of spiritual and theological fellowship among Protestant missionaries in the nineteenth and early twentieth centuries. Meeting in an unfamiliar territory, one will more easily discover the significance of a common heritage. This led to the establishment of the central ecumenical organizations, which came together for the formation of the World Council of Churches (WCC) in 1948, consisting of both Protestant and Greek Orthodox member churches. The Roman Catholic Church was for a long time not part of this development, rather concentrating on solidifying its own trenches through the dogmas concerning the Virgin Mary (conception without original sin, declared to be a dogma in 1854; assumption to heaven, declared to be a dogma in 1950) and the infallibility of the pope (declared to be a dogma in 1870). However, even this church has let go of some its characteristics, like mass in Latin and the withholding of the chalice from lay people, and has developed a positive attitude toward, and some degree of participation in, the ecumenical movement and the WCC. The Second Vatican Council (1962-65) was an important facilitator for this reorientation.

This has created a completely new atmosphere for doctrinal discussions among the churches. For the first time since the Reformation, representatives of the churches have left their trenches and started to discuss doctrine from the presupposition that their own doctrine may after all not be infallible, and that there may be important truths to be learned from the doctrine and experience of the other denominations.

This development has produced several significant documents, some with relevance for all churches, and some produced through bilateral dialogues between different denominations. The most important document with relevance for all churches has been the Faith and Order statement *Baptism, Eucharist and Ministry* from 1982 (Faith and Order is a part of the WCC). Here Greek Orthodox, Roman Catholic, and many Protestant churches together declare something that amounts to a renewal of the vision of unity from the Nicene Creed. The sacraments are unanimously understood as means that God uses to reach us with his grace, and all participating parts agree in discontinuing what may be conceived as rebaptism. Not all Baptists and Pentecostals agree with what this document here says. It is still significant as a serious attempt to solve one of the most divisive practices in Christendom by encouraging churches to mutually recognize each other's baptisms despite continuing disagreement both concerning the understanding and practice of baptism. In 2013, a new document (*The Church: Towards a Common Vision*) was issued and this document may with time be as significant as *Baptism, Eucharist and Ministry* has been.

Protestant churches have been involved in numerous bilateral dialogues. The Leuenberg Concord from 1971 tries to define a new foundation for Protestant union in Europe by settling the dispute between Lutherans and Reformed. The Porvoo Common Statement from 1992 is a similar agreement between the Scandinavian Lutheran Churches and the Anglican Church.

Dialogue documents like these do not solve all problems. Sometimes a reader may be in doubt whether they document real progress toward a deeper unity or the creativity of their writers when it comes to hiding traditional disagreements between imprecise expressions. When they document unity, it does not always materialize in the form of new practices, and the internal relationships between the documents, e.g., between Leuenberg and Porvoo, may be unclear. There is, however, no doubt that they document a willingness to follow the program that is defined as the adequate approach to doctrinal disagreement already in the preface to CA: we should discuss and listen to each other, returning "to one single truth and to Christian concord . . . by correcting whatever has been treated differently in the writings of both parties."[6] This is a complicated process and will undoubtedly take more than one generation. Compared

---

6. Kolb and Wengert, *The Book of Concord*, 31.

to the centuries where nothing happened, apart from the deepening of the trenches, the progress has still been considerable.

However, it is primarily the divisions between the Orthodox and the Roman Catholic Churches, and between the Roman Catholic Church and what for this reason became the Lutheran Church, that are the defining divisions in Christendom. The development regarding these relations is therefore particularly interesting. The relationship between the Orthodox and the Roman Catholic Church has a long and complicated history, which cannot be recapitulated here. There is no doubt, however, that in our time we have seen real progress, even here. In 1965, the pope in Rome and the patriarch in Constantinople formally abolished the mutual condemnations, and since 2006, the incumbents of these offices have met several times. In 2016, the pope and the Russian Orthodox patriarch met for the first time. This has, however, not influenced the attitude of the Orthodox toward the doctrine of papal infallibility, which remains a real stumbling block for them.

After the Second Vatican Council, there have been several dialogues between the Roman Catholic and the Lutheran Churches. Even here, we have seen results, though there is disagreement concerning their significance. From the outset, an important goal was to find a fundament for celebration the Eucharist together. We have yet to succeed in this respect, despite a document from 1978 that documents a wide-ranging agreement concerning the doctrine of the Eucharist. *The Joint Declaration of the Doctrine of Justification* (JD) from 1999 claims something similar for the doctrine of justification. This claim is heavily disputed, though, among other things because its approach to the sixteenth-century debates is deeply problematic. JD investigates whether the "mutual condemnations" from the time of the Reformation may be abolished. However, the problem is not mutual condemnations, but the one-sided Roman Catholic rejection of the Lutheran reform movement despite the catholicity of its criteria for church unity. From a Lutheran point of view, it is also deeply problematic to maintain that there is agreement concerning the doctrine of justification when the Roman Catholics still object to celebrating the Eucharist together. The fact that the Roman Catholic Church still upholds its doctrine of indulgence, which was the starting point of the Reformation, complicates the evaluation of what has actually been achieved through the dialogues.

Methodically more precise is the Catholic–Lutheran dialogue document *The Apostolicity of the Church* from 2007. It succeeds in documenting considerable convergence between the two churches, e.g., in the understanding of the relation between the Bible and the tradition of the church. At the same time, this document does not refrain from specifying where the development has moved in the wrong direction, which often seems close to taboo in an ecumenical context. In this regard, the document both refers to the Roman Catholic unilateral declaration of new dogmas concerning the Virgin and the infallibility of the pope, and the Lutheran acceptance of the ordination of women and same-sex marriage. These problems have not even started to be discussed. The situation is further complicated by the Roman Catholic Church today in some cases defending positions that in the sixteenth century were defended by the Reformers, while representatives of today's Lutheran Churches, partly due to the influence of the Reformed Protestant understanding of tradition, have left them and may defend entirely different positions.

Preparing for the 500th anniversary of the start of the Reformation in 2017, the two churches in 2013 published a little book called *From Conflict to Communion*. This book summarizes the results of fifty years of dialogue and documents that it now is possible to unite behind a common description of the history of the Reformation. Even Roman Catholic church historians now admit there were justified elements in Luther's critique. The question that is not asked is whether there even would have been a Catholic-Lutheran church division if the leaders of the Roman Catholic Church then had said what they say today. The question does not have a definite answer, but that is often the case with good questions.

The ambiguous status of the documents from the dialogue with the Roman Catholic Church is closely related to a methodological problem affecting all dialogues with this church. The ambitions of infallibility inherent in the self-understanding of Roman Catholicism implies that it cannot simply admit to having been wrong in doctrinal matters. There is no doubt that there is considerable distance between the doctrines of justification in the decisions of the Council of Trent and in JD, but the Roman Catholic Church must somehow maintain both. This further complicates the evaluation of the most divisive doctrine of Christendom besides the practice of rebaptising Christians from other denominations, namely the dogma of the pope's infallibility. Today, it is emphasized that the pope is a part of the fellowship of bishops and the entire Catholic fellowship in a way this was not done in 1870. The new openness toward other denominations is a step in the same direction. But the dogma of infallibility is not abolished, and it is unclear how it will be applied in a critical situation.

In a wider perspective, there may be only two ways open for the ecumenical movement. One will either have to argue that the denomination to which one belongs has advantages that imply that the basic model for church unity will have to be found here. Or one will be committed to the vision of unity from the Nicene Creed to the extent that one is willing to discuss all characteristics peculiar to individual denominations. In the latter case, all denominations will probably have to abandon parts of their traditions to comply with the overarching goal of realizing church unity. This goal does not have to be organizational unity. What cannot be abandoned, however, is the goal of full mutual recognition of the validity of each other's ministry and sacraments.

8

Religious experience

Presence and anxiety

BOTH THE BIBLE AND the tradition of the church are important sources for Christian theology. However, both are primarily historically oriented, while Christian theology is primarily interested in reflecting on the encounter with God as a present reality. How do we encounter God today, and how should the experience of this encounter be handled in a methodologically responsible way? That is the subject of this chapter.

Stories of religious experiences are important, both in the Bible and through the history of the church. The Bible contains strong descriptions of divine presence. Reading the story of God's descent to Mount Sinai (Exod 19:16-19), one is not in doubt that this was a powerful experience. In Psalm 18:8-16 we have a similar description of divine presence.

In the Old Testament, it is mainly the prophets who have such powerful experiences. The visions are particularly detailed in the books of Isaiah and Ezekiel (Isa 6; Ezek 10). Normally, however, the prophets experience God's presence as a call to proclaim a specific message (cf. chapter 4). This is a message that pertains to the actual situation and may be provoking for those who receive it. The prophecy may contain predictions of future events, but this is not decisive. Biblical prophecies are not primarily predictions, but applications of the will of God on aspects of the contemporary situation.

We hear of prophets even in the New Testament (Acts 21:9-10; Rom 12:6; 1 Cor 11:4; 12:10; 14:32, 37), but here the ministry of the prophet is different. When Jesus commissions his disciples, he asks them to proclaim what has happened and the significance of these events (cf. chapter 6). The task is not to give new revelations, but to proclaim and explain the revelation that has occurred through the incarnation and the resurrection of Jesus. This must then apply even to New Testament prophecy. It cannot bring anything that questions the ultimate significance of the incarnation and the story of Jesus as the decisive revelation of who God is (cf. John 1:18).

In the New Testaments, it is therefore not only the prophets who experience God's presence. A Christian worship service is, according to the New Testament, always an encounter with the risen one (1 Cor 10:16; 11:29). The experience of the presence of the Spirit through humans confessing their faith (1 Cor 12:3b) and showing divinely induced attitudes (Gal 5:22–23) is also supposed to be real for all Christians. The presence of God in worship and confession has an experiential dimension that is considered essential. There is, however, no description of theophany in the New Testament. The exception is the descriptions of the heavenly worship in Revelations 7, 19, and 21, which resemble the similar descriptions in the books of Isaiah and Ezekiel.

For humans, the encounter with God is not necessarily a happy experience. It can be felt to be both menacing and dramatic. This is repeatedly expressed both in the Old and New Testament. Experiencing the presence of the holy God lets humans be confronted with their sinfulness and inadequacy (Isa 6:5; Matt 8:8; 26:75; Luke 5:8).

This is also reported by those who through the history of the church have been most concerned about the experiential aspect of the life with God, the so-called mystics. Admittedly, they describe the union with God as an ineffable joy. That is the case also with the most important mystic in the New Testament, the apostle Paul (2 Cor 12:1–4). On one's way toward this experience, however, one has to go through an experience of purification and anxiety that is often described as the dark night of the soul. Experiencing union with God is incumbent upon laying off everything that does not belong in this context, and that is a painful experience. This is something even Paul experienced (2 Cor 12:7–10).

In Luther's writings, we meet the experiential dimension of faith in its positive aspect through reflections on what he calls the inner clarity of Scripture (cf. chapter 6). There are two interesting aspects of what he says here. Firstly, he is so intent upon connecting the subjective aspect of faith life to the story of Jesus that he calls it the inner clarity of the Scripture. In Luther's view, this experience is connected with and obtains through meditative interaction with the text of the Bible as the means through which the presence of Jesus manifests itself. Secondly, Luther emphasizes that the experiential dimension of faith is only directly relevant for the individual who is having the experience. Congregational ministry and public proclamation must be grounded in publicly available sources. It is unacceptable to exercise authority based on private religious experiences, as this is something that necessarily leads to abuse of power. This is a critique Luther raised against both charismatic prophets and the hierarchy of the Roman Catholic Church when it referred to its own, uncontrollable sources for theological knowledge (cf. chapter 5). The subjective and experiential dimension of faith is helpful when it comes to discovering and explaining the biblical revelation, but it is only acceptable as ecclesial and social authority through documented and justified exposition of the Bible. Here Luther is renewing a position known from the critique of Gnosticism in the early church.

Luther also knew from his own experience what the mystics call the dark night of the soul. According to Luther, this is an annihilating experience of how one falls short of the measure of perfection the Bible confronts us with, resulting in despair as the dimension of hope fades from reality. He describes is as an experience of hell and may even criticize mystics for having a one-sidedly theoretical approach to this experience.[1] Without having experienced this bottomless anxiety, one does not know what it is. However, with the great mystics Luther also shared the experience that it is from this zero-point God creates the relation of trust that is the essence of the experience of salvation. When all attempts at trusting oneself are burned away, faith can take root in God's own, unchanging love, and this lets one experience an entirely new foundation for one's life.[2]

This overwhelming experience of the fullness of divine love is a life-changing experience, but it is not stable. It is always threatened by the experience of anxiety and will therefore repeatedly have to be regained through interaction with the biblical promises of salvation. We cannot live on the mountain of transfiguration, even if we can easily identify with Peter when he wanted to (Matt 17:4). What we have experienced there, however, is essential when we return to the valley of despair (cf. Matt 17:14).

This experience of life-changing grace and renewal is, in Luther's view, essential in the training of theologians. This is what is expressed through his statement that it is prayer, meditation, and anxiety that create a theologian. Through prayer one opens oneself to the reality of the divine, through meditation one applies the biblical story to oneself, and through anxiety one experiences the struggle with the powers intent on attaching

---

1. Alfsvåg, *Luther as a Reader of Dionysius the Areopagite*.
2. Alfsvåg, *What No Mind Has Conceived*, 209.

one's soul to this-worldly hopelessness and prevent faith from taking root in God's unchangeable love.[3]

In my view, Luther is here addressing something extremely important. When Christian faith has proved to be powerful and resilient in different eras and social contexts, this seems to be closely related to its ability to endure and interpret the experience of hopelessness and God's absence in a meaningful way. When Jesus in his death throes on the cross appropriates the words from Psalm 22:1, "my God, my God, why have you forsaken me?" (Matt 27:46), this experience is implanted in God's own reality. This powerfully expresses faith's capacity for perseverance through crises and tragedies. It has been suggested that this should be seen as a kind of experience-based proof of God's reality. Be that as it may, there is no doubt that this expresses a recognizable faith experience that many find highly relevant.

The experiential dimension of faith is asymmetric. The experience of anxiety is stable in a way the experience of salvation is not. The experience of anxiety is our own, while the experience of salvation is an experience of divine presence founded on the biblical promises of divine grace. From the point of view of Luther and the mystics, it is therefore the experience of anxiety ("Anfechtung") that is the most unambiguous experience of the God-relationship. Sooner or later, the dark night of the soul reaches all of us. The experience of divine light is an experience of being graced, which is a gift one cannot give oneself.

Given this point of departure, divine presence can only be unambiguously experienced through the promises of God's promising presence founded on the apostles' telling of the story of Jesus. This is what is expressed when CA 5 insists that the Holy Spirit effects faith "through the Word and the sacraments as through instruments," and when CA 7 insists that it is agreement "concerning the teaching of the gospel and the administration of the sacraments" that constitutes "the true unity of the church."[4] At the receiving end, this is expressed primarily through the confession of faith (Matt 10:32; Rom 10:9) and obedience. Neither confession nor obedience are unambiguous, though. Nobody fully understands their own motives for doing what they do, and one certainly cannot control the confession and obedience of others. Faith can be confessed hypocritically, and the fruits of the Spirit may not be

---

3. Bayer, *Theology the Lutheran Way*, 33–64.
4. Kolb and Wengert, *The Book of Concord*, 41 and 43.

externally distinguishable from human care with differing motivations and framed in differing perceptions of reality.

Consequently, the dividing line between true and merely apparent believers is therefore something that can never be drawn with confidence. Despite Jesus being very explicit that this is the case (cf. Matt 13:29-30, explained in vv. 38-39), there have through the history of the church been many who have not been satisfied with this. One of them was Pelagius, who wanted an ethics of obedience that was unambiguously verifiable (chapter 5). Augustine rejected this approach and connected the experience of divine presence to interaction with the text of the Bible through the liturgy of the church.

In the Middle Ages, the desire for an unambiguous experience of divine presence was combined with the idea that the church must prepare for a worthy reception of Jesus when he returns to judge the living and the dead. One thus has to establish a purified kingdom of true believers as a preparation for the coming of the Lord. With a reference to the text of the thousand-year kingdom in Revelation 20, this is called postmillennialism, as the return of Jesus is supposed to take place after (post) the thousand years (the millennium). This view can serve as a motivation for spiritual renewal in ways that can have a lot of positive consequences. Both the formation of the mendicant monastic orders (Franciscans and Dominicans) in the thirteenth century and the Protestant foreign missions' movement are examples of postmillennialist renewal movements. As far as the mission movement is concerned, one can here even refer to the words of Jesus (Matt 24:14). But there are also many cases where postmillennialism has caused a demand for unambiguous signs of a true spirituality with disastrous consequences.

At the time of the Reformation, Thomas Müntzer (1489-1525) represented a postmillennialism that was both charismatic and political in character. According to the revelations he claimed to have received, one should, weapon in hand, fight God's enemies and establish the perfect kingdom of God on earth. Political postmillennialism is thus closely related to the idea of holy war (cf. chapter 6). Müntzer's work as a warrior prophet ended in a disaster that confirmed both Roman Catholics and Lutherans in their rejection of his violent and charismatic eschatology. As could be expected from the understanding of revelation found in the Augsburg Confession, this document minces no words in its rejection of postmillennialism (CA 17).

However, modernity's desire for unambiguous, empirical verification (cf. chapter 3) led to the demand for undeniable religious experiences being voiced in a new way. The two great revival movements of the eighteenth century, Methodism in England and Pietism in Germany and Scandinavia, both wanted to answer the quest for an unambiguous experience of God positively. Methodism found this answer in John Wesley's (1703–91) doctrine of sanctification and the second blessing. This second blessing was a strong experience of the presence of the Spirit to which Wesley found references in the New Testament, e.g., in the description of the Pentecostal miracle in Acts 2, but which he also explained from what he had felt and seen within the revival movement. The second blessing was not identical with the experience of conversion from unbelief to faith but presupposed and deepened it.

Pietism had a somewhat different approach. The point of departure was here the struggle for faith the Pietists thought they found both in Luther and others including the Pietist leadership. They had all lived through a process where they went from a feeling of guilt caused by their own sinfulness through the confession of sins to the blissful experience of faith in the reality of reconciliation. This so-called *ordo salutis* doctrine (*ordo salutis* = the order of salvation) was described psychologically in a way that allowed for a precise identification of divine presence.

Common for Methodism and Pietism was the tendency to describe a life in obedience and sanctification casuistically. One claimed to have experiential proof that specific aspects of a so-called worldly way of living necessarily drew people away from faith, either because they were in themselves sinful (disobedience toward one or more of the Ten Commandments) or because they created commitments incompatible with genuine faith (dancing, theatre performances, drinking of alcohol, playing with cards, etc.). One thus found that the progress of sanctification could be measured by the absence of secular entertainment.

This corresponded to a strong demand at the time for experiential proofs for the reality of divine presence. From this point of view, both Methodism and Pietism are successful attempts at proclaiming the Christian messages in ways that are relevant within the context of contemporary culture (contextualization). On the other hand, this implied a change in the understanding of experience from what I have described by referring to Luther and the mystics, in spite of Luther being an undisputed authority for both Methodists and Pietists. Luther's approach anchored the unambiguity of salvation in the biblical promises understood as manifestations of divine unchangeability, thus avoiding the instability of human psychology in this context. When this principle is abolished, specific human achievements are seen as necessary conditions for the realization of salvation. The understanding of salvation thus drifts in the direction of Semi-Pelagianism. In Methodism, it became explicitly Arminian (cf. chapter 5).

Neither is there any justification in church history for the conclusion that the *ordo salutis* pattern is universally applicable. It is here sufficient to refer to the most important of all Christian conversion experiences, the apostle Paul's encounter with Jesus at the outskirts of Damascus. This encounter was not preceded by a spiritual battle. On the contrary, when Paul met Jesus, he was very satisfied with his faith life. The understanding of the need for grace was for him something that came later (cf. 1 Tim 1:15). This shows that different people will experience the path towards faith in vastly different ways. There is no unambiguous psychological pattern here.

Even the casuistic ethics of sanctification (the emphasis on adiaphora) was dependent on the faith experience of specific persons. Renouncement of certain goods is a necessary aspect of a sound spirituality, but the New Testament and the creeds have their reasons for being reluctant towards universal specifications in this respect. In the second part of the Augsburg Confession, it is emphasized that the specifics of renunciations cannot be considered conditions for church unity and made into something absolutely necessary. In Pietism, the understanding of this aspect of the Lutheran confession is unclear at best.

Methodism and Pietism are in many respects constructive movements. They have succeeded in involving lay Christians in work for inner and outer mission in an unprecedented way. This involvement was an effective barrier against the rationalist critique of the Christian faith and went a long way in reducing its influence. Some of the leading theologians, e.g., Schleiermacher, had their background in the revival movement and were clearly influenced by it. At the same time, these movements also left behind a problematic inheritance that is still felt within Protestantism. Their tendency to focus on particular experiences as signs of a genuine faith life has left a lot of people with the feeling that they do not fulfil the requirements for entering the kingdom of God (which is true, but irrelevant). The particulars of the ethics of sanctification have created apparently clear distinctions between those within and those without with their inherent temptations to mutual critique and rejection. While these distinctions have met with a lot of criticism from scholars of theology, it is still a reality in the sense that attempts at raising a debate of ethical issues from a Christian point of view are often understood as an effort to reintroduce the Pietist adiaphora doctrine.

Healing and liberation

In some of the nineteenth-century revival movements, charismatic postmillennialism was renewed in a more radical way than in Methodism and Pietism. This is connected to the fact that during this period, there was a renewed interest in miraculous healings, both within and without Christian congregations. Admittedly, the church's understanding of salvation had never been one-sidedly intellectual. The restored God-relationship includes humans in a reality encompassing all aspects of life. The Old Testament concept of *šālôm*, often translated as "peace," refers to health, welfare, and wholeness in a comprehensive way. Both the Book of Psalms (e.g., Ps 23) and the descriptions of Job before and after his disasters tell us about this. We see the same in the Gospel stories about Jesus, where his compassion for the whole human being is emphasized.

The church considered this a pattern to be followed. The miraculous aspect of the healing ministry was not necessarily accentuated. But it was an important aspect with the ministry of the church that a life in obedience to Jesus included an obligation to care for human needs in general. Praying for the sick did not amount to a promise of recovery. Recovery has many aspects, and when eternity is the frame for its realization, it can be understood in different ways. We are also pointed in this direction by the fact that the New Testament attitude towards suffering is not one-sidedly negative. It can also be seen as one of the challenges that are necessary for faith to grow. This is Paul's conclusion when he had struggled with the problem of a healing that did not happen (2 Cor 12:8–9).[5]

However, this approach was considered insufficient by the representatives of a new kind of healing ministry that we see from the second half of the nineteenth century. They claimed to know the laws of the spiritual realm and to be able to utilize them for the benefit of humans in the same way as technology founded on the new, scientific worldview now was becoming more widespread. In the Christian context, miraculous healings were interpreted within the framework given with Wesley's doctrine of the

---

5. Porterfield, *Healing in the History of Christianity*

second blessing. It was thus seen as the manifestation of spiritual power at the command of the spiritually advanced in a way that fulfilled the New Testament promises concerning prayer in the name of Jesus. The Pentecostal movement, which spread from the beginning of the twentieth century, adopted this way of thinking, adding to it an understanding of speaking in tongues as a similarly unambiguous manifestation of the power of God. At the time of the apostles, the church had grown by means of signs and wonders (Acts 2:43; 5:12; 6:8; 15:12; Rom 15:19; 2 Cor 12:12). According to the Pentecostals, this had evaporated, and they found this lack of signs and wonders as a confirmation that the established churches were spiritually dead. The new manifestations of the work of the Spirit through healing and speaking in tongues, sometimes referred to as power evangelism, proved that church life as known from the time of the apostles again had become a reality. This movement radicalized the Reformed understanding of tradition to the extent that the continuity of the communication of faith through history disappeared entirely.[6]

Neither the Pentecostal movement nor the renewal of Pentecostalism often referred to as the charismatic movement accepted the ideas of the radical faith-healing movement without modifications. Still, there is no doubt that faith healers like Essek W. Kenyon (1867–1948) and Kenneth Hagin (1917–2003) have had a strong influence on parts of Protestantism. They maintain that Jesus vanquished the devil because of his superior knowledge of the laws of spiritual warfare. This knowledge is now placed at the disposal of the believers. By believing like Jesus they will succeed in leading a life liberated from worries concerning health and economy. What is done by the ordinary health services is not criticized, but it is seen as something the truly spiritual do not need.[7]

A further development of this tradition, which calls itself the New Apostolic Reformation (NAR), interprets the manifestations of the Spirit mainly in political categories. Spirit-filled persons should counter the devil's negative influence on society through prayers of power and by filling positions that enables them to promote the work of spiritual powers beneficial for humans. Here, even this aspect of Müntzer's postmillennial vision is renewed. NAR seems to be an important part of the ideological background for the Trump presidency.[8]

6. Harrell, *All Things Are Possible*.
7. McConnell, *A Different Gospel*.
8. Berry, *Voting in the Kingdom*.

There are striking similarities between the faith-healing movement and Gnosticism (cf. chapter 4). In both cases, humans are supposed to achieve a higher level through their knowledge and use of the spiritual laws that faith heroes, first and foremost Jesus, have uncovered. This knowledge is communicated through channels that are unavailable for ordinary people (secret instruction and prophetic messages) and manifests itself in conspicuous ways. One of the implications of this view is that the difference between those with knowledge and those without becomes highly significant.

Jesus commissioned his disciples to proclaim a message of forgiveness of sins (Luke 24:47; John 20:23). Taking this as the yardstick for evaluation, it seems that the faith-healing movement reduces the significance of incarnation and reconciliation, replacing the message of the New Testament with an emphasis on the Spirit's contemporary revelation of new knowledge. Differing from the New Testament, one thus maintains the Old Testament understanding of prophecy. One thus obliterates the anti-gnostic and Reformation-based principle the church should always be led by means of justifiable arguments founded on open and publicly available sources. The charismatic faith healers or NAR-prophets may thus acquire an extraordinarily strong position. The negative implications of this uncontrollable use of power is not something that is seen only in the Müntzer movement in the sixteenth century.

The basic problem represented by the understanding of healing and speaking in tongues as unambiguous manifestations of divinity is that it is hardly compatible with the understanding of reality found in the Bible and the central creeds, according to which there is an absolute difference between God and the world. Taking this as one's point of departure, manifestations of divinity in the world are unambiguously knowable only as connected with the incarnation and its preparations and/or implications, the latter being preaching of the gospel and the administration of the sacraments. Signs and wonders are therefore in the Bible seen as ambiguous phenomena that in themselves create neither faith nor obedience (Exod 7:11; Matt 12:27; Luke 16:31). Nothing communicates God's unchanging love if not qualified by the testimony of the biblical prophets and apostles. This principle cannot be eliminated without undermining the New Testament understanding of the incarnation as the decisive manifestation of divinity.

According to the biblical understanding of creation, God is always present, even if the ambiguous character of our experiences makes this difficult to understand. However, the faith-healing movement seems to find God's presence limited to the instant of the miracle. This thus follows the Nestorian pattern of diving reality in its divine and merely human aspects (cf. chapter 4). One then loses sight of the biblical principle that one draws near to the God who is always there through trials and afflictions. Even for Jesus, the path to resurrection went through the dark night of the soul.

A practical problem created by the healing movement, independent of its presenting itself as connected with the story of Jesus, is that it creates a difference between those who have grasped the spiritual laws and show it through the amount of success in their lives, and those who remain in the dark. The promise of healing for those who believes in a sufficiently strong and correct way will soon be a burden for those who struggle with chronic decease. However, the commandment to always love one's neighbor implies that one should always conduct the ministry of healing in such a way that persons are included in a healing fellowship irrespective of any change in the medical and psychiatric diagnoses.

It is not only the NAR-movement that has renewed the political aspects of Müntzer's postmillennial vision. Even Marxism is looking forward to a perfect, earthly kingdom in a way that can be described as secular postmillennialism. Marxists even explicitly refer to Müntzer as one of their protagonists. Similar dreams of a wonderful future are found in Nazism, transhumanism, and liberalism. This shows that political thought may have distinctly theological aspects. However, neither of these ideologies has adopted anything that corresponds to the New Testament rejection of holy war. They may therefore be used as instruments for political oppression, which has been repeatedly the case. Even secular political ideologies may wage holy war against their opponents.

Marxism has also been employed on specifically theological terms as a means for making the obligation of obedience more concrete, but in a way that is characteristically different from what occurs within the charismatic traditions. In theology inspired by Marxism, one focuses on the fact that humans are caught and oppressed by political structures, which the church, consciously or unconsciously, may support. To be an honest disciple of Jesus therefore implies a willingness to use political analysis and to be involved in political work for the sake of liberating people from oppressive social structures. The starting point of liberation theology was the marginalization and oppression of the poor, but this starting point has been modified and expanded to include the liberation of black and colored people, aborigines, women, homosexuals and other sexual minorities, and the liberation of the earth from humans' oppressive misuse of it.

There is no doubt that liberation theology is right in its emphasis that political structures may be oppressive, and that we by the biblical ideal of *šālôm* are obliged to be conscious of them and strive for their being abandoned. There are situations where the Christian message will not be trustworthy without being accompanied by political action in this way. However, the question that was raised in relation to the understanding of healings and speaking in tongues as manifestations of divine presence must also be raised in relation to liberation theology, where critiques of oppressive structures are similarly understood to be unambiguous manifestations of the divine. To connect divine presence unambiguously to the struggle for and the experience of political liberation may be an over-simplification. Even for a theology of liberation, the unambiguous expression of divine presence must be connected with the story of the incarnation and its contemporary manifestations in the life of the congregation. This gives an irrefutable norm for the effort to thwart oppressive structures while avoiding the danger of this effort being the one and only criterion for true obedience.

Both charismatic and political postmillennialism may go far in dividing people in those who understand and those who do not. This dichotomy is sharpened when one considers those who do not understand to be under the command of the devil. However, Jesus emphasized the obligation to love everybody including our enemies (Matt 6:44) in a way that seems to be a variance with all kinds of dualism. Admittedly, the New Testament finds the work of the evil one to be a reality that manifests itself both in political oppression, persecution, and contempt of God. For this reason, the New Testament encourages the believers to resist this influence (1 Pet 5:8–9) through the confession of sins, proclamation of the gospel, and censure of social oppression and injustice. However, the New Testament does not require the reconfiguration of the political to an arena of spiritual struggle as demanded by the NAR movement and parts of liberation theology. The kingdom of God is not realized through victories in the realm of the political. The understanding of the political as spiritual power struggle undermines the universally inclusive ministry as described in the New Testament and wipes out the distinction between political work and the proclamation of the gospel. Even in this respect, postmillennialism seems to be captured by an understanding of reality that deviates from the biblical one in significant ways.

The life to which Jesus invites us is a good life. The Bible therefore describes it in a way that includes both spiritual bliss and material benefits. However, on biblical terms this must be seen as a sign of divine blessing and not be exchanged from what under all circumstances remains the overall goal, which is the establishment and sustenance of a trusting God-relationship. To avoid our confusing sign and reality, the external signs are sometimes removed. Through such trials, faith grows in steadfastness. This has always been the case, and there is no reason to think it is different today. Christians should therefore serve their neighbors in such a way that trust in God remains the decisive religious experience, irrespective of the external circumstances.

9

Reason as a source of theological knowledge

Proofs of the existence of God?

HUMANS ARE ESSENTIALLY REASONABLE. Reason enables us to analyze the world in ways that have no known parallels. Animals may have advanced knowledge, may communicate, and may establish social fellowships. But they do not seem to discuss their own situation while consciously reflecting on the origin and objective of reality. They may have advanced systems of communication, but do not seem to have philosophical or theological study groups. Humans are thus unique on the earth, and clear signs of such activity anywhere else in the universe have yet to be discovered.

In this book, I have repeatedly maintained that human reason may be understood in two different ways. We may understand reason as a tool for relating in a meditative and reflecting way to a reality that surpasses our capacity for definite knowledge, and to which we therefore can only consistently relate as receivers. In the history of European thought, Plato is the one who thinks through the implications of this perspective in a way that became a point of orientation for subsequent thinkers, and it has been crucial for Christian thought through most of its history. However, it is also possible to choose a more anthropocentric starting point and maintain that reality equals what is thinkable from a human perspective. We have movements in the direction of this point of view in antiquity, but it becomes important for Christian thought through William Ockham's application of this approach. From the late Middle Ages, Christian thought has therefore had to relate to the difference between these paradigms. The era we call modernity, the period from the Enlightenment to the second half of the twentieth century, is characterized by a general preference for Ockhamist anthropocentrism. In chapter 3 and 4, I have discussed some of the challenges this present for the understanding of theology. In this chapter, I will look more closely at the implications for the understanding of reason and its capacity for understanding God and the world. As I have already explained, the Ockhamist paradigm greatly expands the area of precise and experientially demonstrable knowledge. Can this be integrated in the theological project without Christian theology losing its foundation in a creation- and incarnation-based understanding of reality?

The limitation of the Platonic-Augustinian approach concerning the capacity for knowledge of God is well expressed in the work of Anselm of Canterbury (1033–1109). In his book *Proslogion*, the goal is to describe the reality to which he relates in prayer. The world as we experience it is full of phenomena that are both real and thinkable. Examples of such things are the book you now are reading, but also abstract phenomena like courage and moderation. These phenomena have real existence and can be described with understandable concepts. But we also have concepts for phenomena that do not exist, which are made by combining known phenomena in creative ways. We have both gold and mountains, but we have no gold mountains. There are both humans and horses, but no centaurs. However, according to Anselm, the opposite is equally true. There are real phenomena for which there are no adequate concepts. This is the kind of reality he relates to in prayer, Anselm maintains. When we use the word "God," it refers to something real, but we are unable to grasp with our words and concepts what we speak of or address. We do not and cannot know what God is, but God is that than which nothing greater can be conceived. This is a way of explicating the Augustinian tradition of *docta ignorantia* (cf. chapter 3) in a way that precisely addresses the limitation before us.[1]

When, 150 years after Anselm, Thomas Aquinas explains the reference for the word "God," the unthinkable has disappeared. We are on our way to the modern paradigm. There are five ways, Thomas says, we may use to explicate what we refer to when we say "God": He is the first mover, the first cause, necessary existence, absolute measure and the one who organizes the world's purposiveness, i.e., its different elements being made in such a way that they function well in their proper place. In our reflections on the reality of which we are parts, thought needs an absolute point of reference. If the quest for origin or foundation disappears in the fuzziness of pure and undefinable infinity, thought short-circuits and reality is

---

1. Alfsvåg, *What No Mind Has Conceived*, 98–101.

void of meaning. 'God' is the word about the point where the movement of thought toward the infinite is arrested.

Thomas thus stops short of discussing God's own reality. For Thomas, the understanding of God is to be approached through God's relation to the world. This is related to Thomas' primary philosophical sparring partner no longer being Plato, but Aristotle (384–322 BC), whose thought has a more practical, experience-oriented orientation than what is found in his teacher Plato. Neither Aristotle nor Thomas is consistently anthropocentric. However, what Thomas suggests with his five ways is an understanding of God where God's relation to the world is essential for the understanding of God.[2]

The anthropocentric turn in the fourteenth century takes another decisive step. Thomas does not develop a formal proof for God's existence but shows how the word "God" refers to the cause of logically necessary phenomena. Nowadays faith in God is expressed as a problem that logically allows for different answers (chapter 3). This leads to the restructuring of Thomas's five ways as proofs for the existence of God, which differs from the way he conceived them. The world must have a first mover and a first cause. If not, its coming into being becomes unthinkable (the cosmological proof of God's existence). All existence cannot be merely potential; something must exist with necessity. All our evaluations cannot be relative; to be meaningful, they must relate to an absolute standard that ascertains their validity. The well-organized nature cannot be arbitrarily created; it must be structured by a creative intelligence (the teleological proof).[3]

This created the modern tradition of proving the existence of God. Even earlier generations had reflected on God as the Creator and Provider of a well-organized cosmos. However, that had, as in Anselm, been a reflection that considered a faith-based God-relationship the only adequate starting point for a consistent exploration of the world, as God and God's creative act were related to the fact that the world was seen as something that surpassed the human capacity for precise knowledge. When reality is considered equal to the human ability for analyzing it, one necessarily has to ask whether God, from this presupposition, can at all be thought to exist, and the proofs of God's existence are attempts at giving a positive answer to that question.

---

2. Alfsvåg, *What No Mind Has Conceived*, 104–9.

3. Davies, *An Introduction to the Philosophy of Religion*, chapter 3 and 4; McGrath, *Christian Theology: An Introduction*, 155–62.

René Descartes (1596–1650) considered the proofs of God's existence based on Thomas's five ways to be insufficient. He wanted to find a path to unassailable knowledge by doubting everything, including our beliefs about the external world. Proofs of God's existence that take our perception of the world for granted, will then not be helpful. The only unquestionable point of the departure is the fact that I am a thinking subject (*Cogito, ergo sum* = I think, therefore I am). A proof of God's existence can then only be relevant if it proceeds from pure thought, excluding the world of experience. For that purpose, Descartes resurrects Anselm's approach and reconfigures his meditation on divine infinity as a formal proof of God's existence. What in Anselm is *unknowable* reality for Descartes becomes *perfect* reality, and what is perfect cannot lack anything, not even existence. "God" is thus, for Descartes, a concept that refers to the perfect, which then necessarily must exist. If God should have other perfections (omnipotence, omniscience, etc.) but lack existence, God would not be perfect. But since the word "God" refers to the perfect, it does not refer to a phenomenon without existence. Therefore, God necessarily exists.[4]

The proofs of God's existence are doubly problematic. One may question whether the arguments are sound. The conceptual dialectics that here are unfolded will not convince everybody. However, a rejection of the cosmological proof entails the eternity of the world, which also may be a difficult idea. Even more problematic is the rejection of an absolute standard of morality, as this seems to entail a radical relativism, which is difficult to maintain. Dispensing entirely with the idea of truth makes our statements into inchoate utterings of sounds that are only seemingly meaningful. However, even if we find the arguments acceptable, the question of their significance is still unresolved. They can only prove logically necessary principles. The human ability to think then functions as the criterion for reality. But the God to whom we relate in faith is not a logically necessary thought structure, but something analogous to a personal existence who acts, who we can relate to in prayer, and who is never grasped by the human capacity for thought (cf. chapter 3).

This is the reason for the rejection of the proofs of God's existence found in the thought of Descartes's contemporary Blaise Pascal (1623–62). Both Descartes and Pascal were scholars who contributed to the development of modern natural science. However, differing from Descartes, Pascal rejects the methods from natural science when approaching God. To God

---

4. Marion, *Is the Ontological Argument Ontological?*

as manifest through the biblical revelation, one can only relate with the passion of faith. The presuppositions of mathematics and physics are entirely insufficient. In this way, Pascal comes close to a position we met earlier in this book in Luther and Kierkegaard, and like those, he is inspired by Augustine. According to this view, the methods of experience-based science are developed to analyze the relations between created phenomena, and they seem to be relevant in this context. It is, however, a category mistake to think that they are equally adequate for understanding the world's relation to its Origin. This is strongly emphasized by Pascal.[5]

Even Kant was critical of the proofs of the existence of God, but for a different reason and with a more ambiguous conclusion than what is found in Pascal. Kant accepts that the anthropocentrism of modernity implies that our access to reality is closed. We will never proceed beyond an understanding of how the world appears for us according the presuppositions we have been given. The fact that it appears to have a divine origin is therefore insufficient for Kant. He does not share the faith of Aquinas, Ockham, and Descartes in the ability of rational thought to grasp reality. Somewhat reluctantly Kant therefore has to let go even of the teleological proof, which an Enlightenment thinker like Kant tended to evaluate quite favorably. Neither can he accept Descartes's argument concerning the necessary existence of the perfect. For Kant, existence is not a property to be added alongside other properties like size, form, and number, etc. So one cannot argue, as Descartes did, that a perfect being must have the property of existence in order to be perfect.

However, Kant cannot accept the idea of reality without of God. For him, the existence of God is something we must accept from arguments of morality. If there is no heavenly judge to reward the good and punish the evil, Kant's moral universe loses its foundation, and this is an idea he cannot accept. He thus accepts an argument related to the proof from the necessity of an absolute standard for evaluation. While rejecting theoretical proofs of God's existence, he still accepts this moral, practical approach.

The problematic aspect of proofs of God's existence made from the presuppositions of the anthropocentricity of modernity is thus clearly exposed. Both Descartes and Kant need God to balance the accounts of their worldview. God becomes the assistant of humans connecting the dots and pieces of reality. As emphasized by Pascal, this is to turn the relationship between God and humans upside down. It does not make sense to

5. Hunter, *Pascal the Philosopher: An Introduction*.

understand God as the one who fills the gap in the human account of reality. This reduces faith in God to wishful thinking, which is exactly what Feuerbach insists that it is (chapter 3).

However, criticizing this tradition does not entail a conclusion concerning God's reality. As shown by Anselm, this reality must be approached in an entirely different way. In addition, it is still relevant to point to the fact that the rejection of faith in God has both theoretical and practical implications that may be hard to accept. Neither the eternity of the world nor the absoluteness of a human perspective is necessarily an attractive perspective. This does not amount to a logical proof of God's existence. But it shows that faith is not irrational.

Karl Barth maintained that theology should make itself independent of the philosophical debate concerning the rationality of faith in God. Divine revelation should be proclaimed from its own presuppositions without its proponents striving for alliances with philosophical ideas of God. From another starting point, a similar point of view has been promoted by philosophers of religion who take their point of departure from the thought of the Austrian philosopher Ludwig Wittgenstein (1889–1951). He thought that words get their meaning from the context within which they are used. This is also the case with the word "God," which is irreplaceable as a part of the language of prayer and worship, but which does not necessarily make sense outside of this context. The Welsh philosopher D. Z. Phillips (1934–2006) developed this approach into a sharp critique of the proofs of God's existence. "Proof" and "God" belong in different life contexts that should not be confused. Statements about God articulate an approach to reality that is undermined by the attempt at capturing it within the framework of a theoretical understanding of reality.

Barth and Phillips may have a point. Faith in God has its own logic, which is not easily captured from another starting point. That is the reason the criterion of falsifiability cannot be readily applied on statements about God (cf. chapter 3). However, statements of God may still have a content that needs consideration, even outside the context of prayer and worship. Faith in creation is articulated through statements about the origin and connection of all phenomena, and about the conditions for knowledge of reality. If statements about God have no relevance outside the language of worship and liturgy, this universal aspect of the God-relationship disappears. Theological traditions intent on maintaining the integrity of their own thought systems without finding the dialogue with other approaches interesting, are often said to be guilty of fideism (*fides* is faith in Latin). This is a critique that has been found relevant both in regard to Barth's theology of revelation and the Wittgenstein-inspired philosophy of religion.

Divine difference and unknowability—a perspective to which I have repeatedly returned in this book, and which preempts any attempt at proving God's existence—must therefore be combined with universally understandable arguments for the rationality of this approach to avoid theology disappearing into fideism's sealed-off compartment. The position that God is not rationally graspable is a perfectly rational position. I have in this book referred to Neoplatonism as a philosophical tradition that lets us see this point clearly. Two twentieth-century thinkers who, from somewhat different starting points, have approached a similar conclusion are the English literary scholar C. S. Lewis (1898–1963) and the American philosopher of religion Alvin Plantinga (b. 1932). Lewis thought that the ideas of death and resurrection common in many religious myths are important for understanding human approaches to life and the quest for God. The Gospel stories about Jesus have a similar approach to the significance of death and resurrection, but they do not appear to be mere myths. They are far too realistic. Lewis is thus in profound disagreement with Bultmann's program of demythologization (cf. chapter 3). The New Testament depiction of Jesus does not present an obsolete worldview but makes good sense.[6] When Jesus is presented for us in this way, we must either reject, or we must accept that we are confronted by a manifestation of the depths of reality that has no parallel. In the latter case, the story of Jesus is what illuminates everything.[7]

Plantinga for his part agrees to some extent with the critics of the proofs of God's existence. One cannot prove beyond all doubt that God exists. However, the arguments may still contain valuable elements. For instance, Plantinga has tried to reformulate the ontological proof in a way that lets the argument remain valid without being a strict proof. Plantinga's version of the argument seeks to show that either God's existence is *necessary* or it is *impossible*.[8] If he is right, then if one believes that God's existence is *possible* (and even most atheists concede this) then this entails that God *must* exist.[9] Of course, says Plantinga, the atheist could concede this point and simply

---

6. McGrath, *The Intellectual World of C. S. Lewis*.

7. Lewis, *Mere Christianity*, 52.

8 One can see his argument for this claim in Plantinga, *The Nature of Necessity*, ch. 10. Here I simply state his conclusion, not his argument for it.

9. Oppy, *Ontological Arguments*.

argue that God's existence is *impossible*, so God *cannot* exist, and this could be a rational position to take, but it is not the position that atheists usually wish to take. So the argument does not prove that God exists, but for those inclined to think that God *might* exist, it provides reasons to conclude that God *does* exist. This approach is a secondary thought construction that cannot replace faith's life with God in worship and obedience. However, it may still give a hint of the universal relevance of faith in God.

Theology and natural science

Modern natural science developed from explicitly theological presuppositions (cf. chapter 3). Its original goal was to explore and understand the diversity of the experienced world in the same way as someone reading the Bible was exploring and seeking to understand the diversity of divine revelation. However, influence from what I have called the Ockhamist paradigm (nominalism) led both theology and science to adopt more one-sidedly fact-oriented models of knowledge.[10] They were not considered to be in conflict. The idea of a conflict between theology (or religion) and science is a modern construction which is applied anachronistically to periods that did not think in these terms at all. Both Kepler and Newton would have been surprised to be informed they were in a conflict with theology. This is the case even with Galileo. His disagreement with representatives of the Roman hierarchy is regularly interpreted as a sign of a profound disagreement between science and religion that in reality did not exist.[11]

However, fact-based models do contain a possibility of conflict if they disagree in the interpretation of the same facts. After Charles Darwin (1809–82) had presented his theory of the origin of the species in 1859, this theory was framed within a conflict model by representatives of both science and theology. The modern idea of a conflict between science and theology is thus to a large extent created by a specific way of interpreting Darwin's theory of evolution. The theory itself does not demand this interpretation, and neither Darwin nor his critics originally thought in these terms. Darwin was not an atheist, and his critics were not opposing experience-based natural science. Still, it was interpretations of his theory

---

10. Funkenstein, *Theology and the Scientific Imagination*; Harrison, *The Territories of Science and Religion*.
11. Harrison, *The Territories of Science and Religion*, 172–73

that helped create the modern myth of a necessary opposition between theology and natural science.

This is to some extent caused by the theological framework within which the theory of evolution was conceived. It was supposed to be a critique of the teleological proof of the existence of God as presented by the English clergyman William Paley (1743-1805) in his book *Natural Theology* (1802).[12] Here he applies the so-called watchmaker analogy. A watch cannot create itself; it must have an intelligent designer. This must then even apply to nature, which is infinitely more complicated than the finest watch. The argument is problematic, as it presupposes the ability to argue directly from creation to its Creator. One may thus question whether it adequately integrates the absolute difference between the two. In addition, it makes the problem of evil acutely relevant. If God is the demonstrable origin of everything that seems to be good and well organized, what then about the failures and catastrophes? Still, the argument was commonly accepted among the thinkers of the Enlightenment, with Kant as an important (and reluctant) exception.

Darwin's grand idea, developed in *The Origin of Species*,[13] is that the high degree of adaptability in nature could be explained without the idea of a designer. The fact that plants and animals seem to be designed for life in their specific environments should rather be explained from the theory that only those who are well adapted will survive and bring their characteristics to the next generation. Through the generations we thus get accumulations of the qualities that bring an advantage in the struggle for limited resources. This will in time lead to the evolution of new species. This was an audacious theory that, when first suggested, was built on shaky ground. The laws of heredity were yet unknown, the ideas of the age of the earth were faulty, and Darwin did not refer to fossils to defend his theory. But he followed Ockham's principle of looking for simple and unambiguous explanations and let the hypotheses remain as simple as possible. Darwin theory sought to explain how animals could look well designed without there being an intelligent Designer. Appealing to a Designer, based in the teleological proof of God's existence, Darwin considered a complicating hypothesis he did not need. Others had come to similar conclusions, and Darwin's theory therefore gained influence in spite of its shortcomings, which were repeatedly referred to in the ensuing debate.

---

12. McGrath, *Darwinism and the Divine*.
13. Darwin, *The Origin of Species*.

Modern evolutionary biology can now answer many questions Darwin did not even know to ask. The earth is now considered sufficiently old for the plurality of species to evolve. Fossils show that species have appeared and disappeared throughout the history of the earth, and DNA is reused in different species. But scholars have also found the interaction between genetics and environment to be more complicated than what was allowed for in the original version of the theory of evolution. New features are not only created through mutations; even the environment contributes by turning specific features on and off. Formation and evolution of species thus seem to occur in ways that are vastly more complicated than what Darwin could imagine. However, there is no doubt that the biodiversity on earth has changed over time, and that the interaction between heredity and environment is essential both for the formation and extinction of species.

Evolutionary biology has thus come a long way since Darwin. However, it has always carried the burden of the philosophical presuppositions from which it was conceived. It has thus not only inherited the anthropocentricity of modernity but reshaped it in a racist and Eurocentric way.[14] The idea of the survival of the fittest corresponded with and was used as an argument for British and European colonialism. This led to the defense of the "might is right"-principle in Social Darwinism that not only was adopted by Nazism but to a large extent was commonly accepted in the West in the first part of the twentieth century.[15] Today, similar points of view are defended both by transhumanists and others who wants to manipulate human biology to create more advanced humans.[16] The critique of the teleological proof of the existence of God has also survived among those who use evolutionary biology as an argument for atheism as documented by the books of Richard Dawkins (b. 1941) and his partisans. If faith in God is a scientific hypothesis—and Dawkins is seemingly unable to think in other categories—evolutionary biology has falsified it, he claims.[17]

Some have therefore concluded that a consistent defense of faith in God implies that evolutionary biology should be rejected as an erroneous scientific theory. There are two versions of this critique. One is called creationism, which does not only reject evolutionary biology, but even the commonly accepted theories concerning the age of the universe and the

---

14. Dorrien, *Kantian Reason and Hegelian Spirit*, 542–49.
15. Hall, *To Form a More Perfect Union*.
16. Alfsvåg, *Transhumanism, Truth and Equality*.
17. Dawkins, *The God Delusion*; Hart, *Atheist Delusions*.

age of the earth. Creationists maintain that the story in Genesis tell us that the world was created in six twenty-four-hour periods about six thousand years ago, and that this should be accepted as a fact. The other version of the critique is found among the adherents of the principle of Intelligent Design (ID). The ID-adherents accept both the commonly held theory of the age of the earth and that species have evolved over time. However, they differ from the majority of evolutionary biologists by thinking that the existence of an intelligent designer can be demonstrated scientifically. They thus maintain that Darwin's and evolutionary biology's critique of the teleological proof of the existence of God is unacceptable. How should these critiques be evaluated?

Creationism is self-contradictory. Its adherents want to defend a biblical worldview but do it from presuppositions taken from modernity's fact-based approach to reality. The critique I have earlier raised against fundamentalism (chapter 6) is therefore relevant also in relation to creationism.

The ID-movement deserves a more nuanced critique. For reasons I now find it unnecessary to repeat, the teleological proof of the existence of God does not work as proof in a strict sense. We therefore have no reason to criticize Darwin and his disciples for developing theories of biological evolution independent of this proof. However, they may thereby have committed the error of not paying sufficient attention to the most advanced result of biological evolution on earth, which is human consciousness. Questions concerning the adaptability of nature are asked by humans. Biological evolution has thus reached a level where its own product asks questions concerning the process through which it has come into being. Is this merely the result of arbitrary processes to the effect that human consciousness is to be considered an accident? Or is the process, for reasons we (still?) do not understand, organized toward the goal of being able to formulate questions concerning its meaning and significance? If one allows oneself the possibility of playing with the latter possibility, the modern construction of reality as entirely reducible to mathematically describable relations of causality is undermined and replaced by an idea of nature as a self-organized entity striving for complexity and self-understanding. One has thus undermined the Cartesian distinction between the material and the intellectual upon which the cathedral of modernity is founded.[18]

It thus seems as if reflecting on the most significant product of evolution, human consciousness, widens the perspective in ways that

18. Cunningham, *Darwin's Pious Idea*; Hanby, *No God, No Science?*.

undermine the project of modernity. This does not confirm the claim of the ID-movement that God's existence is empirically provable through research on the creative acts through which new species or new organs are conceived. Theirs is still an approach too strongly influenced by the modern fact-based understanding of knowledge, and thus seems to have problems with the idea of God as Creator of and present in all phenomena and all events. God is not more unambiguously present in the successful mutations than in the failures. However, it confirms the claim of the ID-movement that reality as experienced both in everyday life and through the research of natural science cannot be understood without the question about God necessarily being raised. The question cannot be answered through the approach of natural science, but there is no surprise in that. That is the position that has been maintained by theologians and philosophers through the entire intellectual history of Europe.

Biologists rarely take part in discussions of these questions. This proves nothing but their being trapped within the naturalist paradigm within which evolutionary biology was conceived. The problem with this paradigm is that its understanding of evolution never moves beyond the level reached by the more advanced of the animals to the effect that the understanding of the animals is arbitrarily applied even to humans. It follows from these presuppositions that the human is understood as an advanced mammal, the implication of which is that human consciousness is understood as something that is merely supposed to serve the survival of the species. Whether or not it contributes with anything beyond this level is considered uninteresting. This undermines the significance of theoretical knowledge, including evolutionary biology, which in this perspective has no purchase on reality, but can only develop points of view that in the long run are supposed to serve the survival of humankind in the struggle for continued existence. The idea of truth then dissolves, and science can no longer be understood as a quest for establishing and defending justified truths about reality.

The interesting thing is that there is nothing in the research results of evolutionary biology that entails conclusions like this. They are caused by the underlying theological and philosophical presuppositions that govern the interpretations of the results. They claim that the quest for meaning is uninteresting. That this quest is the most advanced, and thus most interesting result of the process under scrutiny falls outside the frames of the paradigm to the effect that it hardly registers.

I have used some pages on the discussion of evolutionary biology because that is where the modern idea of a conflict between theology and natural science originates. To a large extent this is caused by evolutionary biology working from debatable theological presuppositions of which biologists hardly seem to be aware. The same can be said about those who keep the conflict-idea alive from the other side, the creationists and parts of the ID-movement. To the degree that one is aware of these presuppositions, the conflict evaporates. Theology as a discussion of the relationship of humans with God is not dependent on specific theories of natural science. Theology lives well with different theories concerning the origin of the universe, the structure of the atom, the age of the earth, and the evolvement of the species. However, the interpretation of these theories within the grand scheme of things will always reveal the kind of theology the interpreters are working from. Being aware of one's theological assumptions is therefore important for all academic disciplines.

The biblical understanding of God as different from and independent of, but still present in, all that occurs gives a good model for the interpretation of the research of natural science. The model is related to, and can therefore also use concepts from, the Christological debates from the fourth and fifth centuries. This is not an arbitrary parallel; the goal of Christology is to develop a model for understanding God's presence in the world.

According to this model, God and the world are independent of each other ("without confusion"). Understanding God as Creator is therefore not a theory that anything in the world behaves in a specific way. God's work as Creator is therefore not captured by the analysis of cause-and-effect relations between phenomena in the world. Some versions of the teleological proof of God's existence (e.g., Paley's) are struck by this critique.

At the same time, God is present in, with, and under all that occurs ("without separation"). God is not Creator in the sense that he acts at specific points of time, e.g., when new species are created, or when specific prayer requests are fulfilled (cf. chapter 3). God is *always* present. This creates problems, because not everything in the world bears witness to God's goodness. Nevertheless, this is where faith's trust is anchored.[19]

This model ensures free and independent research within the disciplines of natural science, which are not governed by theologically argued assumptions of the how the universe should be. At the same time, the model does not give natural science the privilege of setting frames and

19. Alfsvåg, *Unknowability and Incarnation*.

limits for theological theories. In a similar way, theology is free to ask critical questions both concerning the assumptions of natural science and the theoretical perspectives it uses to interpret and popularize its results. Natural science has been used to defend both racism and an unsustainable exploitation of natural resources. One can thus hardly doubt the necessity of a critical perspective. This critique will always contain elements of theology, because theology is where questions concerning the overall perspective are asked.

An incarnation-based understanding of reality implies the rejection of the conflict model concerning the relationship between theology and natural science. The two should rather meet for critical dialogue and mutual enrichment. Natural science will develop new models to understand how physical, chemical, and biological processes occur and how they have shaped the world we live in. In, with, and under all of it, the gaze of faith sees the presence of the Creator who is the Origin of all there is without being identical with any of it.

10
Goals and means for theological work

THE STARTING POINT FOR this book was the question of the relation between content and method in theological work. Because theology is an academic discipline pursued by persons searching for knowledge, theology is subject to the same criteria for openness concerning sources and arguments as other academic disciplines. However, theology investigates a relation, namely the relation between God and humans, that differs from all other relations. This gives theology its defining characteristics, which in this book have been discussed through chapters on God as Creator, divine revelation, the human as the receiver and communicator of divine revelation, and the Bible, tradition, experience, and reason as the sources of theological knowledge.

In this final chapter, I will summarize some of the conclusions. Seeing God as Creator and Origin of all there is does not make God and the world into opposites. Thinking that way implies understanding God from the assumptions of the created. God and the world are simply profoundly different. Experience and observation are still important sources of knowledge, both concerning God and the world. The relation to God is important both as a precondition for the possibility of experience-based knowledge, and because it qualifies specific slices of reality, the biblical writings, and the tradition of the church as particularly important sources of theologically relevant knowledge.

Theology is not a discipline primarily interested in isolating specific facts and getting to know them as precisely as possible. As I have repeatedly made aware of through this book, this is a model of knowledge closely associated with a specific era in the history of Western thought, the era of modernity. The model has its strength within the confines of natural science, though it has its limits, even in this context. For theology, it has only limited relevance. This does not mean that theology is uninterested in knowledge.

GOALS AND MEANS FOR THEOLOGICAL WORK

The improvement of our knowledge concerning the content of the Bible and the history of the church, of the history of theology and the history of thought is always advantageous. However, the goal of theology is not to acquire a body of knowledge concerning a fixed list of topics. The goal is to understand which topics are important and why, and acquire a method for working with these topics in a meaningful way. Theology is thus a discipline where the questions are more important than the answers.

Gadamer's hermeneutics shows us this in an interesting way (chapter 6). It explains how we can work with classical texts to the effect that they may widen and shape our perception of reality. For this work there is no list of fixed and correct answers. We will not know the outcome in advance when we give ourselves to be reinterpreted by texts with a potential for changing our lives. But, as Gadamer also makes us aware of, we never approach this encounter unbiased and without presuppositions. As a student of theology one encounters the texts of the Bible with the knowledge that these texts were collected to communicate the person and work of Jesus, who in these texts is presented as the one who shows us who God is. As Jesus makes us aware, this encounter may lead us to places we did not intend to go (cf. John 21:18). This is something we cannot change. It is given with the distinctive character of the sources with which theology occupies itself.

This amounts to an awareness of the elements to be contained in the theological working process for this process to capture and change us. To make these elements easy to remember, they can be summarized the as the four "L"s that describe the laws of living local congregations. They are important in this context because local congregations are essential for the education of theologians.

Liturgy. In this context, the word "liturgy" describes active participation in the spiritual life of the church, both concerning the common worship service and what Jesus is thinking of when he tells you to "go into your room and shut the door and pray to your Father who is in secret" (Matt 6:6). The liturgy may not always be the same, even if there are reasons for giving some preference for the way of worship the church has practiced since antiquity. The significance of the liturgy is that it takes us into the room where an incarnational spirituality unfolds. In worship, we encounter God in the shape of word and sacrament. This does not remove us from the world but renews our understanding of the world as the place where God is. From worship as fellowship centered on divine presence there is a path to fellowship with everybody and everything God has created.

Learning. A Christian worship service is an encounter with the risen one. This encounter has a specific cognitive content, which is contained in the biblical writings and summarized in the creeds. This is the main reason the acquisition of theological knowledge is important. However, this knowledge can never be abstracted from the way it is communicated. It can only be communicated through the story of Jesus and the concrete manifestations in baptism and the Lord's Supper that Jesus, according to this story, has bequeathed to us. Therefore, the priority of liturgy before learning is not coincidental; theology always starts from the liturgy. Theology is reflection on the life of faith as it is lived.

As the study of theology has been focused on the academic context, theologians have tended to misunderstand this. They have repeatedly, particularly under modernity, thought of theological learning as something that can be abstracted from the means of communicating it and studied separately. It is as if a musician were to learn music only by studying the scores or by discussing the aesthetic value of Beethoven's symphonies. Important though it may be, it does not in itself produce any music. Good theology is only created where an active faith life grows through the encounter with new knowledge and intellectual challenges.

The primacy of liturgy does not make learning and doctrine uninteresting. Worship has an intellectual center: the encounter with the incarnated and risen one. This creates the intellectual challenges that are the subjects of the chapters of this book. Christian theology has a cognitive identity throughout all its manifestations in different times and cultures. To express this identity anew with fidelity toward the continuity of the faith tradition and sensitivity toward the contemporary context is the standing challenge for all theologians.

Leadership. Working with theology academically should qualify for leadership in the church. Schleiermacher understood this and made it a central aspect of his model of the study of theology (cf. chapter 6). The ability to communicate well, to think strategically, specify the goals and motivate others to work for the same goal are important qualities for a theologian. This is also an argument that the acquirement of theoretical knowledge should not be abstracted from the context within which it is supposed to unfold. Knowledge about how to handle personal relationships is important when one is intent on creating fellowships where everybody cooperate from a common vision. When Jesus was teaching his disciples, he also paid attention to this aspect. However, when he was formulating his final mandate on the day of his resurrection, he was more interested in theology than in the psychology of human relationships. The overall goal is to include humans in the realm of salvation (Luke 24:47); the decisive elements are baptism and instruction. We may assume this to be a valid priority even today.

Lay persons. Ecclesial leadership should take care to not develop in a way that makes people into mere respondents. The goal is to create an enduring incarnational spirituality that will let all members of the congregation see all of reality as anchored in the creative activity of God. This will never obtain if the members are passive observers who occasionally drop in to have some instruction from the theological expert. One can only reach this goal when everybody, irrespective of whether they are experts in theology or not, stands together in wanting to be taught and informed by what God gives.

In spite of the significance of learning, hierarchy, and authority, Christian faith therefore has provocatively strong elements of the egalitarian and the democratic. It places all humans, irrespective of competence and qualifications, on the same level before God. This is the reason both for our infinite value and for our falling short of the divine ideal. There are periods in the history of the church where the theological experts forgot this and consciously or unconsciously thought the class of theological experts to be closer to God than other people. As Jesus made us aware in his sharp critique of the Pharisees, who were the theological experts at that time, the people of God will never benefit from this way of thinking. In relation to God, we are all receivers. D. T. Niles (1908–70), a Methodist minister from Sri Lanka, said that sharing the gospel is like "one beggar telling another beggar where to find bread."[1] We will never proceed beyond this principle.

The four "L"s may be combined and summarized in a fifth, but then we must use Latin: ***Lex orandi lex credendi.*** This quotation is, in its original version, found in Prosper of Aquitaine (390–455), a younger contemporary of Augustine.[2] A free translation is: Your faith and theology are determined by the way you pray. Good working habits and a certain persistence are important qualities for a prospective theologian. But a sound and regular prayer life is even more important. Theology is not a spectator sport.[3] One

---

1. Niles, *That They May Have Life*, 51.

2. Lange, *Lex Orandi Lex Credendi*.

3. Borrowed from Warburton, *Philosophy: The Essential Study Guide*, who insists that philosophy is not a spectator sport.

will never get to know divine presence just by reading about it. Faith life is first and foremost practice, and faith practice is first and foremost a life in prayer. The Book of Psalms was Jesus's prayer book and has remained the most important prayer book through the history of the church. Praying the Psalms with the entire Christian church is still the most important path into the mysteries of a life of faith.

In the first chapter of this book, I wrote that one would benefit from having a certain knowledge of the Bible and of the history of theology, philosophy, and science. Some of chapters discuss problems that require a certain level of academic competence to be fully comprehended. In this last chapter, I have tried to return to a more practical level. Irrespective of the amount of knowledge required and the level of abstractness of the arguments, the goal is to contribute to a practical life of faith that is relevant both for the learned and the unlearned.

Søren Kierkegaard understood that. He is arguably the most insightful and influential theologian from the tradition of Scandinavian Lutheran theology. But he was well aware that the pinnacle of abstraction is not where you find the depths of faith. I will therefore let him have the final word: "One does not reflect oneself into Christianity but reflects oneself out of something else and becomes more and more simple, a Christian."[4] The fundamental reality of faith life is a simple relation of trust, but there is a lot that may prevent us from experiencing it. The task of theology is to let these obstacles disappear.

---

4. Kierkegaard, *Writings*, 22,7 (*On My Work as an Author*, 1851).

Bibliography

Alfsvåg, Knut. "The Centrality of Christology: On the Relation between Nicholas Cusanus and Martin Luther." *Studia Theologica* 70 (2016) 1–17.
———. *Christology as Critique: On the Relation between Christ, Creation and Epistemology.* Eugene, OR: Pickwick, 2018.
———. "God's Fellow Workers: The Understanding of the Relationship between the Human and the Divine in Maximus Confessor and Martin Luther." *Studia theologica* 62 (2008) 175–93.
———. "Luther as a Reader of Dionysius the Areopagite." *Studia Theologica* 65 (2011) 101–14.
———. "Postmodern Epistemology and the Mission of the Church." *Mission Studies* 28.1 (2011) 54–70.
———. "'These Things Took Place as Examples for Us': On the Theological and Ecumenical Significance of the Lutheran Sola Scriptura." *Dialog* 55 (2016) 202–9.
———. "Transhumanism, Truth and Equality: Does the Transhumanist Vision Make Sense?" *Theofilos* 7 (2015) 256–67.
———. "Unknowability and Incarnation: Creation and Christology as Philosophy of Science in the Work of Nicholas Cusanus." *International Journal of Systematic Theology* 21.2 (2019) 141–56.
———. *What No Mind Has Conceived: On the Significance of Christological Apophaticism.* Studies in Philosophical Theology 45. Leuven: Peeters, 2010.
The Apostolicity of the Church: Study Document of the Lutheran-Roman Catholic Commission on Unity. Minneapolis: Lutheran University Press, 2006.
Augustine. "Confessions." https://faculty.gordon.edu/hu/bi/ted_hildebrandt/spiritualformation/texts/augustine_confessions.pdf.
Ayres, Lewis. "Patristic and Medieval Theologies of Scripture." In *Christian Theologies of Scripture: A Comparative Introduction*, edited by Justin S. Holcomb, 11–20. New York: New York University Press, 2006.
Baptism, Eucharist and Ministry. World Council of Churches, 1982. Available from https://www.oikoumene.org/en/resources/documents/commissions/faith-and-order/i-unity-the-church-and-its-mission/baptism-eucharist-and-ministry-faith-and-order-paper-no-111-the-lima-text.
Bayer, Oswald. *Theology the Lutheran Way.* Translated by Jeffrey G. Silcock and Mark C. Mattes. Grand Rapids: Eerdmans, 2007.
Berger, Peter L. *The Desecularization of the World: Resurgent Religion and World Politics.* Grand Rapids: Eerdmans, 1999.

BIBLIOGRAPHY

Berry, Damon. "Voting in the Kingdom: Prophecy Voters, the New Apostolic Reformation, and Christian Support for Trump." *Nova Religio: The Journal of Alternative & Emergent Religion* 23.4 (2020) 69–93.

Bettenson, Henry, ed. *Documents of the Christian Church.* 3rd ed. Edited by Chris Maunder. Oxford: Oxford University Press, 1999.

Brink, Gijsbert van den. *Philosophy of Science for Theologians: An Introduction.* Frankfurt: Lang, 2009.

Broadie, Alexander. "Duns Scotus and William Ockham." In *The Medieval Theologians,* edited by G. R. Evans, 250–65. Oxford: Blackwell, 2001.

Bultmann, Rudolf. *New Testament and Mythology and Other Basic Writings.* Philadelphia: Fortress, 1989.

The Church: Towards a Common Vision. World Council of Churches, 2013. Available from https://www.oikoumene.org/en/resources/documents/commissions/faith-and-order/i-unity-the-church-and-its-mission/the-church-towards-a-common-vision

Cunningham, Conor. *Darwin's Pious Idea: Why the Ultra-Darwinists and Creationists Both Get It Wrong.* Grand Rapids: Eerdmans, 2010.

Darwin, Charles. *The Origin of Species by Means of Natural Selection, or the Preservation of Favoured Races in the Struggle for Life.* London: Penguin, 1977.

Davies, Brian. *An Introduction to the Philosophy of Religion.* Oxford: Oxford University Press, 2003.

Dawkins, Richard. *The God Delusion.* Boston: Houghton Mifflin, 2006.

Dorrien, Gary. *Kantian Reason and Hegelian Spirit: The Idealistic Logic of Modern Theology.* Malden, MA: Wiley-Blackwell, 2013.

Farnell, F. David, ed. *Vital Issues in the Inerrancy Debate.* Eugene, OR: Wipf and Stock, 2015.

Feuerbach, Ludwig. *The Essence of Christianity.* Translated by George Eliot. Stilwell, KS: Neeland Media, 2012.

Flew, Antony. "Theology and Falsification." Philosophy of Religion. https://www.qcc.cuny.edu/socialsciences/ppecorino/phil_of_religion_text/CHAPTER_8_LANGUAGE/Theology-and-Falsification.htm

Frei, Hans W. *The Eclipse of Biblical Narrative: A Study in Eighteenth and Nineteenth Century Hermeneutics.* New Haven, CT: Yale University Press, 1975.

From Conflict to Communion: Lutheran-Catholic Common Commemoration of the Reformation in 2017. Leipzig: Evangelische Verlagsanstalt, Bonifatius, 2013.

Funkenstein, Amos. *Theology and the Scientific Imagination from the Middle Ages to the Seventeenth Century.* Princeton, NJ: Princeton University Press, 1986.

Gadamer, Hans-Georg. *Truth and Method.* Translated by Joel Weinsheimer and Donald G. Marshall. 2nd rev. ed. London: Continuum, 2004.

Gerson, Lloyd P. *Ancient Epistemology.* Cambridge: Cambridge University Press, 2009.

Glanzberg, Michael. "Truth." Stanford Encyclopedia of Philosophy. https://plato.stanford.edu/entries/truth/.

Hahn, Scott W., and Benjamin Wiker. *Politicizing the Bible: The Roots of Historical Criticism and the Secularization of Scripture 1300–1700.* New York: Crossroad, 2013.

Hall, Amy Laura. "To Form a More Perfect Union: Mainline Protestantism and the Popularization of Eugenics." In *Theology, Disability and the New Genetics,* edited by John Swinton and Brian Brock, 75–95. London: T. & T. Clark, 2007.

Hanby, Michael. *No God, No Science? Theology, Cosmology, Biology.* Oxford: Wiley-Blackwell, 2013.

BIBLIOGRAPHY

Harrell, David Edwin. *All Things Are Possible: The Healing and Charismatic Revivals in Modern America*. Bloomington, IN: Indiana University Press, 1975.

Harrison, Peter. *The Territories of Science and Religion*. Chicago: University of Chicago Press, 2015.

Hart, David Bentley. *Atheist Delusions: The Christian Revolution and Its Fashionable Enemies*. New Haven, CT: Yale University Press, 2009.

Henry, John. "Religion and the Scientific Revolution." In *The Cambridge Companion to Science and Religion*, edited by Peter Harrison, 39–58. Cambridge: Cambridge University Press, 2010.

Hunter, Graeme. *Pascal the Philosopher: An Introduction*. Toronto: University of Toronto Press, 2013.

Hyman, Gavin. *A Short History of Atheism*. London: I. B. Tauris, 2010.

Hägglund, Bengt. *History of Theology*. Translated by Gene J. Lund. St. Louis, MO: Concordia, 2007.

Ichikawa, Jonathan Jenkins, and Matthias Steup. "The Analysis of Knowledge." Stanford Encyclopedia of Knowledge. https://plato.stanford.edu/entries/knowledge-analysis/

Joint Declaration on the Doctrine of Justification. 1999. Available from http://www.vatican.va/roman_curia/pontifical_councils/chrstuni/documents/rc_pc_chrstuni_doc_31101999_cath-luth-joint-declaration_en.html.

Kierkegaard, Søren. *Writings*. Translated by Edna and Howard Hong. 27 vols. Princeton: Princeton University Press, 1980–2000.

Kobusch, Theo. "Nominalismus." In *Theologische Realenzyklopädie*, edited by Gerhard Müller, 589–604. Berlin: de Gruyter, 1994.

Kolb, Robert, and Timothy J. Wengert, eds. *The Book of Concord*. Minneapolis, MN: Fortress, 2000.

Kuhn, Thomas. *The Structure of Scientific Revolutions*. 2nd ed. Chicago: University of Chicago Press, 1970.

Lange, Dirk G. "Lex Orandi Lex Credendi." In *The Cambridge Dictionary of Christian Theology*, edited by Ian A. McFarland, 276–77. Cambridge: Cambridge University Press, 2011.

Lewis, C. S. *Mere Christianity*. London: Collins, 1986.

Leuenberg Agreement. Available from http://www.leuenberg.net/leuenberg-agreement.

MacIntyre, Alasdair. *After Virtue: A Study in Moral Theory*. London: Duckworth, 1985.

Marion, Jean-Luc. "Is the Ontological Argument Ontological? The Argument According to Anselm and Its Metaphysical Interpretation According to Kant." In *Flight of the Gods*, edited by Ilse N. Bulhof and Laurens ten Kate, 78–99. New York: Fordham University Press, 2000.

Mathison, Keith A. *The Shape of Sola Scriptura*. Moscow, ID: Canon, 2001.

McConnell, D. R. *A Different Gospel: A Historical and Biblical Analysis of the Modern Faith Movement*. Peabody, MA: Hendrickson, 1988.

McGrath, Alister E. *Christian Theology: An Introduction*. 25th anniversary, 6th ed. Hoboken, NJ: John Wiley & Sons, 2017.

———. *Darwinism and the Divine: Evolutionary Thought and Natural Theology*. Oxford: Wiley-Blackwell, 2011.

———. *Historical Theology: An Introduction to the History of Christian Thought*. 2nd ed. ed. Oxford: Wiley-Blackwell, 2013.

———. *The Intellectual World of C. S. Lewis*. Oxford: Wiley-Blackwell, 2013.

BIBLIOGRAPHY

Milbank, John. *Theology and Social Theory: Beyond Secular Reason.* Oxford: Blackwell, 1990.
Murphy, Nancey C. *Theology in the Age of Scientific Reasoning.* Cornell Studies in the Philosophy of Religion. Ithaca, NY: Cornell University Press, 1990.
Nietzsche, Friedrich. *On the Genealogy of Morality: A Polemic.* Indianapolis: Hackett, 1998.
Niles, Daniel T. *That They May Have Life.* New York: Harper and Brothers, 1951.
Okasha, Samir. *Philosophy of Science: A Very Short Introduction.* New York: Oxford University Press, 2002.
Oppy, Graham. "Ontological Arguments." https://plato.stanford.edu/entries/ontological-arguments/.
Pannenberg, Wolfhart. *Theology and the Philosophy of Science.* London: Darton, Longman & Todd, 1976.
Plantinga, Alvin. *The Nature of Necessity.* Oxford: Clarendon, 1974.
Plato. *Complete Works.* Edited by D. S. Hutchinson and John M. Cooper. Indianapolis: Hackett, 1997.
Popper, Karl. *The Logic of Scientific Discovery.* 2nd ed. London: Routledge, 2002.
Porterfield, Amanda. *Healing in the History of Christianity.* Oxford: Oxford University Press, 2005.
Porvoo Common Statement. 1992. Available from https://www.anglicancommunion.org/media/102178/porvoo_common_statement.pdf
Schaff, Philip, ed. *The Creeds of Christendom.* 3 vols. Grand Rapids: Baker, 1977.
Schweitzer, Albert. *The Quest of the Historical Jesus.* London: SCM, 2000.
Stanford, Kyle. "Underdetermination for Scientific Theory." Stanford Encyclopedia of Philosophy. https://plato.stanford.edu/archives/win2017/entries/scientific-underdetermination/.
Steiger, Johann Anselm. "The Communicatio Idiomatum as the Axle and Motor of Luther's Theology." *Lutheran Quarterly* 14 (2000) 125–58.
Taylor, Charles. *A Secular Age.* Cambridge, MA: Harvard University Press, 2007.
Tyson, Paul. *Returning to Reality: Christian Platonism for Our Times.* Eugene, OR: Cascade, 2014.
Warburton, Nigel. *A Little History of Philosophy.* New Haven, CT: Yale University Press, 2011.
———. *Philosophy: The Essential Study Guide.* London: Routledge, 2004.
Zimmermann, Jens. *Hermeneutics: A Very Short Introduction.* Oxford: Oxford University Press, 2015.

Index of Names

Abraham, 79
Alfsvåg, Knut, 26n2, 27n3, 28n5, 37n14, 38n16, 44n2, 52n6, 64n5–6, 65n7, 69n8, 83n6, 103n1–2, 115n1, 116n2, 123n16, 126n19
Anselm of Canterbury, 115–17, 119
Aquinas, Thomas, 30, 115–18
Aristotle, 17, 116
Arius, 43–47, 51–52, 68
Arminius, Jacobus, 65
Athanasius, 44–47, 58
Augustine, 27–30, 34, 36, 57–63, 65–67, 69, 81, 105, 118, 131
Ayres, Lewis, 81n4

Barth, Karl, 55, 66–67, 86–88, 119–20
Bayer, Oswald, 104n3
Beethoven, Ludwig van, 130
Berger, Peter, 1n1
Berry, Damon, 109n8
Bettenson, Henry, 60n3
Brink, Gijsbert van den, 21n9
Broadie, Alexander, 29n6
Bultmann, Rudolf, 31–32, 120

Calvin, Jean, 52, 65–67, 70
Caputo, John, 67–68
Comte, Auguste, 32–33
Copernicus, Nicolaus, 16
Cunningham, Conor, 124n18

Darwin, Charles, 15, 20, 121–24
Davies, Brian, 116n3
Dawkins, Richard, 123

Derrida, Jacques, 67–68
Descartes, René, 117–18
Dilthey, Wilhelm, 87
Dorrien, Gary, 123n14

Einstein, Albert, 16
Erasmus of Rotterdam, 63, 81
Eunomius, 44–46

Farnell, F. David, 85n8
Feuerbach, Ludwig, 32, 34–38, 119
Flew, Antony, 20–21, 23, 36
Frei, Hans W., 83n7
Freud, Sigmund, 15, 20, 32–33
Funkenstein, Amos, 121n10

Gadamer, Hans-Georg, 87–89, 129
Galilei, Galileo, 30, 121
Gerson, Lloyd P., 18n5
Glanzberg, Michael, 10n2
Gregory of Nyssa, 44–46, 51, 68

Hägglund, Bengt, 4n4, 44n1, 48n4, 59n2, 62n4, 78n3, 91n1
Hagin, Kenneth, 109
Hahn, Scott W., 81n5
Hall, Amy Laura, 123n15
Harnack, Adolf von, 79–80
Harrell, David Edwin, 109n6
Harrison, Peter, 121n10–11
Hegel, Georg Wilhelm Friedrich, 53–54
Henry, John, 30n8
Hyman, Gavin, 30n8

INDEX OF NAMES

Ichikawa, Jonathan Jenkins, 9n1
Irenaeus of Lyon, 79, 91

Jesus, 21–22, 31, 41–50, 52, 56, 58–61,
 63, 74–83, 85–86, 89–89, 93–94,
 101–2, 104–5, 107–13, 120,
 129–32
Job, 108

Kant, Immanuel, 52–54, 118, 122
Kenyon, Essek W., 109
Kepler, Johannes, 30, 121
Kierkegaard, Søren, 37–38, 54–55, 118,
 132
Kobusch, Theo, 29n7
Kolb, Robert, 21n8, 45n3, 92n2, 93n3,
 97n6, 104n4
Kuhn, Thomas, 16–18, 21–22, 34, 67, 87

Lange, Dirk G., 131n2
Lazarus, 47
Lewis, C.S., 20n6, 120
Luther, Martin, 11, 22, 30, 51–52, 55,
 62–67, 69–70, 81–82, 93, 99,
 102–4, 106, 118

MacIntyre, Alasdair, 31n9
Marcion, 78–79, 80, 88
Marion, Jean-Luc, 68, 117n4
Marx, Karl, 32–33, 53
Mary (mother of Jesus), 47, 49, 96
Mathison, Keith A., 94n5
Maximus Confessor, 65
McConnell, Dan R., 109n7
McGrath, Alistair, 4n4, 27n4, 73n1,
 116n3, 120n6, 122n12
Milbank, John, 31n9
Müntzer, Thomas, 105, 109–111
Murphy, Nancey C., 20n7

Nestorius, 47
Newton, Isaac, 13, 17–18, 30, 121
Nietzsche, Friedrich, 33–35
Niles, Daniel Thambyrajah, 131

Ockham, William, 29–30, 34, 36, 53, 114,
 118, 122

Okasha, Samir, 4n4
Oppy, Graham, 120n9

Paley, William, 122, 126
Pannenberg, Wolfhart, 20–21, 32, 35, 54
Pascal, Blaise, 117–18
Paul (apostle), vii, 26–27, 31, 36, 39, 45,
 59–60, 63, 75–77, 84, 91, 102,
 107–8
Pelagius, 58–61, 63, 105
Peter (apostle), 75–76, 103
Phillips, Dewi Zephaniah, 119
Philo, 26
Plantinga, Alvin, 120–21
Plato, 1, 18, 25, 26n1, 28, 34–36, 114, 116
Plotinus, 26
Popper, Karl R., 14–15, 20, 32, 35
Porterfield, Amanda, 108n5
Proclus, 26
Prosper of Aquitaine, 131

Schaff, Philip, 48n5, 93n4
Schleiermacher, Friedrich, 84, 86–87,
 107, 130
Schweitzer, Albert, 85, 87
Socrates, 25
Stanford, Kyle, 15n4
Steiger, Johann Anselm, 64n6
Steup, Matthias, 9n1

Taylor, Charles, 31n9, 52n7
Tertullian, 48
Thomas (apostle), 44
Tyson, Paul, 53n8

Vincent of Lérins, 91–92, 94

Warburton, Nigel, 4n4, 131n3
Wengert, Timothy J., 21n8, 45n3, 92n2,
 93n3, 97n6, 104n4
Wesley, John, 106, 108
Wiker, Benjamin, 81n5
Wittgenstein, Ludwig, 119–20

Zimmermann, Jens, 87n10
Zwingli, Ulrich, 52, 93

Index of Subjects

adoptionism, 43
anabaptism, 94
Anglican Church, 95, 97
anxiety, 62–63, 101–7
anthropocentrism, 34, 68, 114–16, 118, 123
apophaticism, see negative theology
Apostles' Creed, 42
Arianism, 43–46, 51, 92
Arminianism, 65–66, 70
atheism, 1, 31–35, 120–21, 123
Augsburg Confession (CA), 92–93, 95, 105, 107

baptism, 57, 59, 69, 80, 92, 130
    of children, 93–94
Baptism, Eucharist and Ministry, 97
Baptist Church, 95, 97
Bible, 4, 25, 57, 73–89
biblicism, 78, 95

canon, 75, 82, 91
Calvinism, 52, 65
catholicity, 90–95
church fathers, 25–27, 46, 53, 57, 65, 82
church tradition, 4, 93–94
clarity of Scripture, 80–86, 102–3
communicatio idiomatum
    (communication of properties), 49, 52, 54
Confessio Augustana, see Augsburg Confession

contemporary context, 4, 83, 86, 101, 106, 112, 130
Councils
    in Nicaea 325, 44
    in Constantinople 381, 44, 46
    in Chalcedon 451, 48–50
    in Trent 1545–63, 66, 83, 93, 99
creation, 3, 24–38, 43, 50, 59, 78, 92, 128
creationism, 123–24, 126
critical rationalism, 14–15, 20

Darwinism, 121–23
deduction, 13
docetism, 43

ecumenical movement, 96–100
election, 59–66, 70
Enlightenment, 52, 83, 114, 122
equality of humans, 33, 131
experience, 4, 101–13
Eucharist, see Lord's Supper
evolution, 123–25

falsification, 14, 20–21, 32, 36, 52
faith, 3–4, 21, 31, 38, 42, 46, 51, 58, 61, 64, 70, 75, 82, 92, 94, 103–4, 106, 116, 118, 121, 130
fideism, 120
forgiveness, 74, 110
fundamentalism, 8, 85, 87, 124

Gnosticism, 43, 90

INDEX OF SUBJECTS

God,
    absence of, 104
    presence of, 37, 46, 50–52, 61, 81–82, 85–86, 88–89, 101–6, 112, 129, 132
    existence of, see proof
    infinity of, 27–28, 40, 43–45, 50–51, 54, 64, 68, 115–17
    unknowability of, 24–31
grace, 30, 58–64, 97, 103–4, 107
    prevenient grace 62

healing, 70, 108–11
hermeneutics, 84, 87–89
historical-critical Bible scholarship, 83, 85–86, 88
homooúsios, 45

idolatry, 25, 40
incarnation, 3, 40–56, 82, 92, 126–27
induction, 12
ineffability, 51, 68, 102
inerrancy, 85, 87
Intelligent Design (ID), 124–26
Islam, 1, 41

Joint Declaration of the Doctrine of Justification (JD), 98–99
justification of knowledge, 9, 12–19

knowledge, 2, 9–23, 69–70, 83, 128, 130

liberation theology, 89, 111–13
liturgy, 44, 80, 105, 119, 129
Lord's Supper, 52, 68, 93, 95, 98, 130
logic, 13, 44, 46, 61
logical positivism, 13–14, 19
Lutheran Church, 66, 95–99

merit, 62, 65
Methodism, 65, 70, 95, 106–7
Middle Ages, 19, 51, 81, 105, 114
modernity, 38, 52–53, 66–67, 83
monasticism, 57–58, 63, 105
monophysitism, 47

mysticism, 65, 102–4, 106

natural science, 121–27
negative theology, 27–28, 34, 50
Neoplatonism, 41, 43, 120
Nestorianism, 47–49, 65
New Apostolic Reformation (NAR), 109–12
Nicene Creed, 45–46, 50, 92, 95

obedience, 58–60, 64, 66–68, 75, 77–78, 104–6, 108, 110–12, 121
Ockhamism (nominalism), 114–15, 121–22
Old Testament, 74–80
ordo salutis, 106–7
Orthodox Church, 26, 95

paradigm change, 17, 22, 30–31
patripassianism, 49
Pelagianism, 59–61, 92
Pentecostalism, 65, 70, 95, 97, 109
philosophy, 19, 26–28, 52, 84–87, 114–21, 124–25
philosophy of science, 2, 4, 13–18, 23
Pietism, 66, 70, 106–8
Platonic-Augustinian tradition, 29–30, 34–36, 53, 115
Platonism, 25–28, 33, 53
pope, 93, 95, 98
    infallibility of, 96, 99–100
postmillennialism, 105, 108–9, 111–12
postmodernity, 67–68
prayer, 36–37, 56–58, 103, 109, 115, 117, 119, 131–32
probability, 37
promise, 40, 50, 80, 90, 94, 103, 107–9, 111
proof of God's existence, 114–21
    cosmological, 116
    moral, 118
    ontological, 117, 120–21
    teleological, 116, 122–23
prophecy, 39–40, 101–2

Protestantism, 31, 52–54, 66, 70, 83–87, 96–97, 107, 109

Quadriga, 81

reason, 4, 26, 51, 114–21
Reformation, 22, 30, 51, 62–63, 66, 83, 92, 94–96, 98–99, 105
Reformed Church, 65, 77, 83, 94–97, 99, 109
relationship with God (soteriology), 3, 19, 37, 56–70, 77–80, 92, 95, 103–4, 106, 108, 131
revelation, 3–4, 22–24, 39–55, 61, 64, 67–70, 80, 82, 86, 92, 101–3, 119–21
rhetoric, 57
Roman Catholic Church, 30, 52, 66–68, 85, 93, 95–99, 103, 105, 121

sacraments, 58, 62, 65, 77, 92, 94, 97, 100, 104, 110, 129
    See also baptism and Lord's Supper
scholasticism, 22

scientific revolution, 12, 30
Semi-Pelagianism, 62, 64–66, 70, 107
sin, 59–62, 92, 106
spirituality, 56–70
synergism, 62, 81

Tanakh, 74
theotókos, 47
theory of evolution, 15
Trinity, 42, 92
truth, 10–12, 17–19, 22–23, 35, 37, 46, 67, 117, 125
two-nature Christology, 48–50, 54–55, 64, 95

ubiquity of Jesus, 50
unknowability, 27–29, 36, 53, 63

verification, 13–14
via moderna, 29

wisdom Christology, 41
worship, 26, 57, 73, 75, 95, 102, 119, 129–30

www.ingramcontent.com/pod-product-compliance
Lightning Source LLC
Chambersburg PA
CBHW050828160426
43192CB00010B/1939